LYDIA DAVIS

LYDIA DAVIS
A STUDY

PAUL McDONALD

GREENWICH EXCHANGE
LONDON

Greenwich Exchange, London

First published in Great Britain in 2019
All rights reserved

Lydia Davis
© Paul McDonald 2017

This book is sold subject to the conditions that it shall not, by way of trade or otherwise, be lent, resold, hired out or otherwise circulated without the publisher's prior consent in any form of binding or cover other than that in which it is published and without a similar condition including this condition being imposed on the subsequent purchaser.

Printed and bound by www.imprintdigital.com
Typesetting and layout by Jude Keen Ltd, Kent
Tel: 07949 644825

Cover image of Lydia Davis © John D. and
Catherine T. MacArthur Foundation,
reproduced under Creative Commons Licence.

Greenwich Exchange Website: www.greenex.co.uk

Cataloguing in Publication Data is available
from the British Library.

ISBN: 978-1-910996-16-4

for Sammy

ACKNOWLEDGEMENTS

Some of this material appeared in the form of a paper delivered at the *Short Fiction: Co-texts and Contexts* conference organised by KU Leuven Department of Literary Studies, Leuven, Belgium, May 4-6, 2017. I would like to thank the organisers of that conference, and members of the European Network for Short Fiction Research for their comments and insights. I would also like to thank Alison Reed for sharing her perceptive thoughts on Davis's stories.

CONTENTS

1	Introduction	11
2	Lydia Davis: Biography	13
3	Literary Breakthrough: 'The Thirteenth Woman'	15
4	Influences on Lydia Davis	21
5	Lydia Davis and Postmodernism	25
6	Obsession and Uncertainty in 'Story'	28
7	Obsession and Uncertainty in 'The Fears of Mrs Orlando'	32
8	Lydia Davis and Micro Fiction	36
9	The Art of the Micro Story: 'The Judgement'	39
10	The Art of the Micro Story: *Can't and Won't*	41
11	The Art of the Micro Story: 'The Old Vacuum Cleaner Keeps Dying on Her'	43
12	The Art of the Micro Story: 'Away from Home'	45
13	Identity, and the Instability of the Self: 'In a House Besieged'	47
14	Identity, and the Instability of the Self: 'What She Knew'	50
15	Lydia Davis and Humour	52
16	Lydia Davis and Puns	56
17	The Process of Writing and 'The Center of the Story'	59

18	The Process of Writing and 'What Was Interesting'	63
19	Lydia Davis and Reading: 'The Letter'	67
20	Lydia Davis and Reading: 'Foucault and the Pencil'	71
21	Lydia Davis and Intertextuality: 'Southward Bound, Reads *Worstward Ho*'	74
22	Lydia Davis and Intertextuality: 'Kafka Comes to Dinner'	78
23	Lydia Davis, Intertextuality and Translation: 'The Walk'	80
24	Lydia Davis, Intertextuality and Translation: 'Marie Curie, So Honourable a Woman'	82
25	Lydia Davis, Intertextuality and Translation: Found Stories in Flaubert	84
26	Lydia Davis and the Lived Experience: 'St Martin'	86
27	Lydia Davis and the Lived Experience: Found Material	90
28	Lydia Davis and the Lived Experience: Letters of Complaint	93
29	Recycled Experience: Lydia Davis's Dreams	96
30	Lydia Davis and Zen: 'New Year's Resolution'	99
31	Lydia Davis and Zen: 'The Cows'	103
32	Lydia Davis and Zen: 'Collaboration with Fly' and 'Sitting with My Little Friend'	106
33	*The End of the Story*	108
34	Structuring the Story of *The End of the Story*	110
35	*The End of the Story* and the Impossibility of Truth	112
36	*The End of the Story* and the Philosophical Novel	115
37	Conclusion	118
38	Selected Bibliography	121
	Endnotes	125

1

Introduction

LYDIA DAVIS IS ONE OF THE most innovative and stimulating authors working in the world today. Despite the fact that her status as a fiction writer is founded on only six books – one novel and five collections of stories – she is seen as hugely influential by critics, and her immense global reputation continues to grow. The aim of this volume is to show why this is the case. It offers a context for her work, demonstrating her alignment to contemporary cultural phenomena like postmodernism, and revealing her pioneering innovations in the field of flash fiction. It begins by exploring her background and influences, then goes on to discuss some of her key stories, addressing her principal themes and preoccupations, and revealing her concern with issues such as identity, language, obsession, and, above all, the processes of writing. It is her interest in the latter that has led some commentators to describe her as a 'writer's writer', but she is much more than this. As one of the great prose stylists of our time, Davis's aesthetic deserves close scrutiny, and this book demonstrates the central role of humour and minimalism in her writing, together with how her work as a translator impacts on her fiction. Ultimately it reveals Lydia Davis as an intellectually engaged, philosophical writer whose work interrogates the human condition in totally original, intensely illuminating ways.

2

Lydia Davis: Biography

LYDIA DAVIS WAS BORN IN NORTHAMPTON, Massachusetts in 1947 into an academic, literary family. Her father, Robert Gorham Davis, was a professor of English at Columbia University, and her mother, Hope Hale Davis, a fiction writer and memoirist who published in *The New Yorker*. They were both left-wing radicals (her father was even questioned by the notorious House Committee on Un-American Activities), and the literary and intellectual elite were regular visitors to their home, including critics such as Lionel Trilling and Edward Said, and renowned writers like Grace Paley and Erica Jong. It was music rather than literature that attracted Davis as a child – she practiced both the violin and the piano – and music has remained an interest throughout her life; indeed, Dana Goodyear in her 2014 interview with Davis reports that, in her mid-60s 'Davis, unexpectedly, plays tin whistle.'[1] She did find time to write in her youth, however, and in recent interviews has spoken about how her childhood diary reveals her as a precocious author who, in her own words, wrote very well, and who took herself 'very seriously as a potential writer.' It seems she had an obsession with the structure and style of sentences, and even at the age of 12 and 13 held herself 'to a very high standard' in her prose compositions.[2] Scrupulous attention to the arrangement of words, and the formal quality of sentences is evident throughout Davis's career, and characterises her writing.

As a student Davis attended Barnard College, although she doesn't seem to have been particularly attentive, preferring instead to accompany her then boyfriend, Paul Auster, to his lectures at Columbia. She travelled to France with Auster in the early 70s, first to Paris, then later to the South of France where the two worked as caretakers in an eighteenth-century farmhouse – this is an experience that both of them write about in later life, Davis in her stories, Auster in his memoirs. The two survived mainly by working as translators, a job that has occupied Davis for much of her life. As Jonathan Evans notes, the pair collaborated on several translation projects, including book length works, such as Jean-Paul Sartre interviews, and Georges Simenon's novel, *Aboard the Aquitaine*.[3]

Davis and Auster found it hard to survive in France and returned to the States in 1974, deciding to marry. Along with their translation projects, both worked on creative material – Auster was writing mainly poetry, while Davis focused on short stories. Neither found immediate acclaim for their creative writing, and at this stage both were still experimenting with form, and working to find a voice.

3

Literary Breakthrough: 'The Thirteenth Woman'

DAVIS STRUGGLED TO FIND A FORM that suited her as a short story writer, and most of her early attempts were unsuccessful. This changed when she came across the work of the American prose poet, Russell Edson, and became inspired by his technique. Edson's poems often read like strange little stories, with an emphasis on narrative rather than language and description. For this reason Davis says that she prefers to call Edson's pieces 'stories', as opposed to 'poems', and this is the term she uses to describe her own work. In several interviews Davis has spoken about how reading Edson's genre-defying pieces opened her eyes to the possibilities of the short form.[4] Her first story in this new Edson-influenced style was called 'The Thirteenth Woman', written in 1974. It is such an important, breakthrough piece that it is worth citing here in full:

'The Thirteenth Woman'
In a town of twelve women there was a thirteenth. No one admitted she lived there, no mail came for her, no one spoke of her, no one asked after her, no one sold bread to her, no one bought anything from her, no one returned her glance, no one knocked on her door, the rain did not fall on her, the sun never shone on her, the day never dawned for her, the night never fell for her; for her the weeks did not pass, the years did not roll by; her house was unencumbered, her garden unattended, her path not trod upon, her bed not slept in, her food not eaten, her clothes not worn; and in spite of all this she continued to live in the town without resenting what it did to her.[5]

The outsider figure will become familiar in Davis's fiction, as will the detached tone of voice detectable here. 'The Thirteenth Woman' is similar to Edson's prose poems in that its emphasis is on narrative rather than language or description, which, as suggested, makes us inclined to call it a story rather than a poem. However, the language still has a poetic feel, particularly in its precision and repetition: it accumulates details in two beautifully balanced sentences, particularly the second, which is masterly in its phrasing. Like many of her later stories, it blurs the distinction between poetry and story; indeed, Davis is one of the few writers to appear in both *The Best American Short Stories*, and *The Best American Poetry* volumes. Certainly this was a breakthrough piece for her, so much so that she calls it her 'first seminal story' [quoted in Goodyear, 2014]. It made her aware of the potential of the short form, and she followed it with more stories of a similar style, setting herself the goal of writing two per day. 'The Thirteenth Woman' became the title story of her first collection, *The Thirteenth Woman and Other Stories*, published in a limited edition in 1976 by Living Hand Press. This book was effectively self-published, Living Hand Press being an arm of a little magazine, *Living Hand*, that she co-edited with Auster (they also published Auster's first poetry collection, *Unearth* in 1974).

A year after the publication of *The Thirteenth Woman*, Davis and Auster moved to an old house in Dutchess County, where their son Daniel was born in 1977. The pair separated eighteen months later, and after the divorce Auster relocated in Brooklyn with a new wife, the novelist Siri Hustvedt. Davis herself eventually moved to a house nearby her ex-husband in order to facilitate access between father and son. She published another small press collection of stories in 1983, *The Story and Other Stories* (The Figures Press), before publishing her first full collection, *Break it Down* in 1986. Printed by Knopf, this was her first book from a mainstream publisher, and it collects together thirty-five stories, including several from the two earlier books (Evans, 2). In 1995 Davis published her only novel to date, *The End of the Story*, and followed this with three more full-length short story collections: *Almost No Memory* (1997), *Samuel Johnson is Indignant* (2001), and *Varieties of Disturbance* (2007).

The more Davis published the more her reputation

began to grow, particularly among critics and fellow writers. *Break it Down* was a PEN/Hemingway Award finalist in 1986; she later won the Whiting Award for fiction in 1988, the Lannan Literary Award for Fiction in 1998, and was a National Book Award finalist in 2007 for *Varieties of Disturbance*. As suggested in the introduction, despite this success, Davis was considered something of 'a writer's writer' [Goodyear, 2014], admired as an original prose stylist, but of little interest to the broader reading public. This began to change after the publication of her *Collected Stories* in 2009, a book bringing together her first four full-length story collections. There is a sense in which the weight of Davis's significance becomes more apparent when her stories are viewed as a single body of work: their range, variety, and profundity is arguably more striking when they are collected together. Her global reputation was secured when this collection won the International Booker Prize in 2013, one of the highest profile literary awards in the English-speaking world. Since then she has continued to produce the type of stories for which she has become famous, publishing her most recent collection to date, *Can't and Won't* in 2014.

Alongside her original stories, Davis continues to work as a translator, having translated over twenty books so far. Most notable are Marcel Proust's *Swann's Way* (2002) and Gustave Flaubert's *Madame Bovary* (2010), which was widely celebrated, and has become a bestseller. Throughout the course of her life she has also taught creative writing at a number of institutions, including the University of Albany, SUNY, and New York University, where she was Lillian Vernon Distinguished Writer in Residence, 2012. She currently lives in upstate New York with her husband, the painter Alan Cote, where she continues to write and translate.

At the time of writing she is working on a number of projects, one of which involves the translation of work in languages of all the countries that have translated her. I mention this because it speaks of Davis's commitment to the idea of herself as an international writer, and her desire to engage with the global literary community: she is deeply interested in, and often feeds off, other writers from all nationalities and cultures. It also speaks of her openness to intellectual challenges. She has spoken in several interviews, for instance, of attempting to learn Norwegian solely through the translation of Dag Solstad's 400-page epic, *The Insoluble Epic Element in Telemark in the Period 1591-1896*. She was drawn to this particular book – that some critics have deemed 'unreadable' – because she sees Solstad as an uncompromising writer, who has the courage of his convictions; importantly, this is exactly how she perceives herself. In one interview she explains that she was drawn to Solstad's writing because she shares his philosophy: 'Do exactly what you want, that's my idea. Some will love it and some will hate it, and that's alright.'[6] Davis identifies with Solstad because he follows his own instincts as a writer, regardless of fashion or commerce, which is true of Davis herself. As will be seen, she is one of the great innovators of modern literature, always willing to test the boundaries of narrative.

4

Influences on Lydia Davis

WE HAVE SEEN HOW DAVIS WAS influenced by Edson, and there are several other American writers who could be seen as significant in her development. When she was young she was inspired by her reading of Henry David Thoreau, for instance, and she also took a writing course with the American short story writer, Grace Paley. But Davis has also spoken about the heavy influence of European writers such as Samuel Beckett and Franz Kafka, as well as the many writers she has translated over the years. Arguably it is European rather than American writing that has had the more noticeable impact on her work. One of the things she admires about Beckett, for instance, is his ability to address complex issues, including abstruse philosophical concepts, in compelling, readable ways. As she says in one interview:

> It always seemed to me that [Beckett] would take very complex philosophical ideas and play them out in a simple

> way with his characters and their actions. So he might take a complicated mathematical concept and play it out with a character [...] Sometimes you read very complex language that either is not making any sense at all or is expressing something fairly simple but dressing it up with complex language. So I've always been a little mistrustful of complex language.[7]

As will be seen, Davis's stories often make difficult philosophical problems relevant to everyday experience, finding interesting and relatable ways of dramatising them, as Beckett does in novels such as *Watt* (1953). And despite the often profound themes, she employs a very lucid and accessible prose style, always free of jargon and polysyllabic words. As a consequence Davis's stories are occasionally viewed as simple, with their complexity and depth overlooked. Because many of her stories are extremely short, they are always in danger of being dismissed as slight, particularly when they are viewed in isolation, outside the broader context of her oeuvre. This danger is perhaps compounded by the internet, where her work is pervasive. While the new media has helped bring her to a wider audience, it tends to disseminate only her shortest pieces, and there is a risk of her being seen exclusively as a miniaturist, or a gimmicky author of micro stories. Her experiments in micro fiction, and her mistrust of complexity, should certainly not be equated with triviality. The comparison to Beckett is apposite in that she, like him, produces work of huge intellectual substance.

In addition to Beckett's penchant for the philosophical, her stories are also sometimes like Beckett's in that they feel cut off from specific times and locations: as Dan Chiasson suggests, some of her stories, 'belong to a class ... made up of all things isolated in time or space ... Beckett's characters on a desolated stage'.[8] One of the things that typifies Davis's stories, for instance, is her tendency not to name characters, or to be specific about locations, and this can sometimes give them an abstract, timeless feel.

So the influence of Beckett is clear, and she also makes direct reference to his writing in some of her fiction, as we shall see. This is true too of Franz Kafka, whom she alludes to specifically in the story, 'Kafka Cooks Dinner', and who is also a significant influence. For instance, there are some similarities between her shortest fictions, and Kafka's short pieces, such as his Parables and Paradoxes – in fact Davis herself suggests that 'they may have planted the idea' for her own experiments in miniature forms.[9] We will also see how Kafkaesque themes and humour feature quite heavily in her work.

As a French scholar and translator of the language, Davis has also been influenced by a host of French novelists. In various interviews she talks about the importance of the French nouveau roman, for instance, and avant-garde writers like Robbe-Grillet and Michel Butor.[10] Reading of this kind underpins Davis's interest in the possibilities of narrative, and her own willingness to experiment with form. She clearly enjoys experimentation both as a reader and as a writer. Another influence among French writers is Marcel Proust, whose work she has translated to high acclaim. In an interview with William Skidelsky she suggests it is 'Proust that she holds responsible for turning her into a miniaturist', maintaining that her move to the shortest narrative forms was a response to her experience of translating him:

> 'I started writing the one-sentence stories when I was translating Swann's Way,' she recalls. 'There were two reasons. I had almost no time to do my own writing, but didn't want to stop. And it was a reaction to Proust's very long sentences. The sheer length of a thought of his didn't make me recoil exactly – I loved working on it – but it made me want to see how short a piece of fiction could be that would still have a point to it, and not just be a throwaway joke.'[11]

She embraces the miniature as a response to translating Proust's labyrinthine sentences, and seems to see concision almost as a challenge: she is interested in testing the boundaries of form, experimenting with the possibilities of succinctness and meaning. Her translation work has influenced her in numerous ways, and we will see how this is particularly true of her more substantial projects like the Proust novel, and later her work on Gustave Flaubert.

5

Lydia Davis and Postmodernism

DESPITE THE INFLUENCE OF MODERNIST WRITERS such as Kafka, and late modernists like Beckett, when critics categorise Davis's fiction they sometimes call her a postmodernist. This term usually refers to art that began to emerge following WWII, and which developed some of the preoccupations of modernism. In the early twentieth-century modernism had questioned assumptions about how the world can be represented in art. In the wake of ideas from thinkers like Charles Darwin, Karl Marx, Friedrich Nietzsche, Sigmund Freud, among many others, the world had become a more complicated place: such thinkers challenged our understanding of ourselves, and how we relate to society, and it was increasingly hard to have faith in traditional ways of depicting the world, such as realism. Artists responded by reflecting these uncertainties, which can be seen, for instance, in the disjointed canvases of Picasso, the fragmented collage poetry of T.S. Eliot, and the stream-of-consciousness narratives of James Joyce and Virginia Woolf. In part, then, modernism emphasises subjectivity, privileging the individual perspective over the possibility of consensus reality. Postmodernism takes these concerns a stage further. Postmodern art begins to question the possibility of any kind of certainty, and particularly the idea that truth can be accessed or expressed via language. Many postmodernist writers were influenced by the theories of people like Jacques Derrida and Roland Barthes, who stress the arbitrariness of language, and its status as an abstract system that does not have any fixed relationship with the world it purports to represent. The extreme implication of such theories is that, in a sense, language only ever produces fiction. Other theorists, such as the psychoanalyst Jacques Lacan, show how language informs our unconscious, impacting on our identity, with the implication that human beings are also constantly in flux, rather than fixed and integrated entities, and we too are, in a sense, fictional. For postmodernists, we are cut off from reality, unable to truly know the world, or ourselves. The first phase of postmodernist fiction is usually associated with the work of American authors like John Barth, William H. Gass, and Richard Brautigan, whose writing responds to such thinking. This writing is often very self-conscious or metafictional in tone, sceptical of its own ability to make meaningful statements about reality, always underlining the fictional nature of any assertion it seems to make. As will be seen, Davis often exhibits exactly this quality: language isn't something that can be relied upon in Davis's world, and while her heroes often crave certainty, they are usually frustrated in that regard. In keeping with the spirit of postmodernism, Davis's writing seems to stress the impossibility of accessing or articulating the truth, even though her characters are often obsessed with the idea of doing so.

6

Obsession and Uncertainty in 'Story'

AN EARLY PIECE THAT DEPICTS JUST such a preoccupation with truth and uncertainty is 'Story', which first appeared in *The Story and Other Stories* in 1983, then later in *Break it Down* (1986). This is narrated by an unnamed woman concerned with the fidelity of her lover, and specifically whether or not he is telling her the truth about his meeting with an old girlfriend. The lover is due to visit the narrator at home, but when he phones telling her he cannot make it, she drives to his apartment. There's no answer when she knocks, so she leaves a note. When she phones him later in the evening he tells her that he has been to the movies with his ex-girlfriend, and that he will call her back:

> I wait. Finally I sit down and write in my notebook that when he calls me either he will then come to me, or he will not and I will be angry, and so I will have either him or my own anger, and this might be all right, since anger is

always a great comfort, as I found with my husband. And then I go on to write, in the third person and the past tense, that clearly she always needed to have a love even if it was a complicated love. [*Collected Stories*, 3]

The narrator here seems to require emotional engagement of any kind: if she cannot have an '[un]complicated love', then even 'anger' offers some comfort for her. The move to the third person as she writes in her notebook is particularly interesting. We assume that the speaker is still writing about herself, but she seems to want to take a step back from her immediate experience in order to analyse it. This is typical of Davis's narrators who are very often seen to reflect on their own reflections, so-to-speak, or to 'watch themselves' think about their world. As Jonathan Evans writes, her stories often focus, 'not on the events of their narrative, but on the character's interpretation of those events.' [*The Many Voices*, 4]. There is a degree of distance in her tone when she moves to the third person, then, and a sense that she is removing herself from the moment – she removes herself from the emotional turmoil that her suspicions create, to be free to ponder the cause of her problem. In 'Story' the narrator interprets her own obsessiveness as an expression of her need for love; she feels that she needs love, despite the painful and bewildering complexity of the emotion. Her use of the word 'clearly' in the extract suggests that she has some confidence in the validity of this interpretation: she believes that she knows what motivates her; in other words, she believes that she knows something about herself and her world. As the story moves on, however, we are forced to question how much she actually does or can know.

When her lover returns her call later that evening they have an argument, and he contradicts himself so much that she hangs up and continues to write in her notebook. However, by this time, the anger that she assumed might offer consolation fails to do so: 'it no longer seems true that anger is any kind of comfort'. [*Collected Stories*, 4] So she moves from a position of certainty (that 'anger is always a great comfort') to a position where this no longer seems true. Just as the truth about her lover is hard to establish, so the truth about herself seems elusive.

She calls her lover back again to apologise but there's no reply, so she decides to drive to his apartment once more, despite the fact that it's past midnight and she needs to leave for a trip at 5am the next day. By this stage we see that the speaker is very obsessive, particularly about the truth of what her lover tells her. She is obsessed with establishing facts – as her use of words like 'clearly' and 'always' suggest – she thinks that such a thing as certainty exists, and appears to crave it. When she arrives at his apartment he doesn't invite her in, but meets her outside, embracing her and apologising for the ruined evening. He confesses that his ex-girlfriend is in his apartment, but only because 'there is something troubling her and he is the only one she can talk to about it'. [*Collected Stories*, 5] The speaker doesn't understand what this means, but tells us that 'I try to figure it out', going on to list the various possible permutations of what could have happened that evening between her lover and his ex. The problem with establishing the facts is that her lover has lied to her in the past, and this makes it difficult to believe him. The story closes with her assessment of why she wants to know the truth anyway:

> I want to know it if only so that I can come to some conclusion about such questions as: whether he is angry at me or not; if he is, then how angry; whether he still loves her or not; if he does, then how much; whether he loves me or not; how much; how capable is he of deceiving me in the act and after the act in the telling. [*Collected Stories*, 6]

As her desire for truth relates to abstract, unquantifiable emotions like anger and love, we begin to see that there are no answers to her questions: certainly there are no absolute truths to be had. Even if she *could* establish the literal truth of what her lover tells her – which she cannot because she can't trust him – this wouldn't bring answers to the questions she poses: 'whether he still loves her … how much; whether he loves me … how much'; it is difficult to imagine how the existence of love can be objectively established, let alone measured. Despite the narrator's detailed reflection on her predicament, then, she appears oblivious to these fundamental, epistemological problems, and the fact that answers simply aren't possible. When the story ends we can only assume that her obsessions will continue unabated.

7

Obsession and Uncertainty in 'The Fears of Mrs Orlando'

ANOTHER EARLY STORY ABOUT THE OBSESSIVE search for truth is 'The Fears of Mrs Orlando', one of the few Davis tales where the central character is actually named. Here the title character appears to be suffering from paranoia, following a number of assaults. We are not sure about the validity of these assaults because there is a suggestion that they may be exaggerated, or even completely fabricated. Indeed, when she claims to suffer another assault, her daughters are sceptical, and so are we. We witness the moment of this so-called 'assault' in the story: Mrs Orlando approaches her car after a shopping trip downtown, and has the impression that a man hiding beneath it grabs her ankle and demands that she drops her purse and walks away. She does so, but the purse never moves from where she drops it. Because the purse doesn't move, and there is no sign of the assailant when she looks back at the car, we wonder if the assault is in her head. Certainly 'Her daughters do not believe her story', and while Mrs Orlando 'is outraged by their disbelief' [*Collected Stories*, 9], it is hard not to share their scepticism. Though the event has just been presented to us by the narrator, it is impossible to say whether or not an 'assault' of any kind actually happened, or whether we have merely shared an incident created by Mrs Orlando's febrile imagination.

A few days later Mrs Orlando runs into a group of people clustered around something on a beach. When she investigates, it turns out to be a young man's corpse, and she joins the onlookers 'absorbed' by the spectacle. When she relates this incident to her daughters on the telephone, she excitedly tells it over and over. Again her daughters are 'uneasy because she becomes so excited each time she tells the story'. [*Collected Stories*, 10] Over the next few days Mrs Orlando's paranoia increases – she claims to receive an obscene phone call, and thinks someone has broken in to her home because things seem to be missing. When she locates the missing items 'in an odd place', we are once more made to wonder about her state of mind. In the closing lines her paranoia increases to such an extent that:

> she stays inside and just talks on the phone, keeping her eyes on the doors and windows and alert to strange shadows, and for some time after this she will not go out except in the early morning to examine the soil for footprints. [*Collected Stories*, 11]

As in 'Story' we have an instance of the obsessive desire for truth, and in the story's closing image we again see the futility of this. Our sense of its pointlessness is augmented by our understanding of the kind of person Mrs Orlando is. We are told, for instance, that while she is 'frightened by her own ignorance', the information she craves most of all relates to 'crime and disaster'. In other words, she is 'avid' for information that will increase her paranoia, which in turn will feed her obsessive need for more information – more so-called truths – in a never-ending cycle. As with the narrator of 'Story', the desire for truth becomes an unhealthy obsession; the mistake for both characters is to assume that such a thing exists, at least insofar as it might ameliorate their trauma. We saw how the narrator of 'Story' uses terms like 'clearly' and 'always', suggesting the illusion of certainty; similarly we are told that Mrs Orlando 'feels most comfortable talking to lawyers because every one of their words is endorsed by the law' [*Collected Stories*, 7], which again reflects a desire for indisputable truth, and a misguided belief in its existence.

We can see how this scepticism toward the accessibility of truth is in keeping with postmodernism, as described above, and such uncertainty is typical of Davis. Philosophical questions concerning what can be known of the world inform both stories – both have an epistemological focus, interrogating what it's possible to understand about reality. In 'Story' we see the absurdity of thinking that abstract concepts such as love can be addressed in terms of truth, while in 'Orlando' we see how the protagonist's personality dictates her attitude to truth, and a self-destructive compulsion to embrace illusion in the absence of truth.

8

Lydia Davis and Micro Fiction

'STORY' AND 'ORLANDO' ARE BOTH APPROACHING conventional short story length (around 2000 words), but of course many of Davis's stories are much shorter, falling into the category of 'sudden fiction' (below 1500 words), 'flash fiction' (below 750 words), and 'micro fiction' (below 150 words).[12] Indeed, some of her stories run to less than 100 words, and some are shorter still, barely a sentence long. There has been speculation about whether some of these count as stories at all, and it really depends on what definition of 'story' one employs. It is sometimes hard to discern the elements of character and conflict usually considered essential to stories, particularly in her shortest texts. Sometimes readers need to do a lot of work themselves in order to make sense of – or make a story of – the little bit of information Davis gives us in a narrative. They must work to create a context in their imagination for what sometimes appear as limited or fragmented statements.

However, like the best short story writers, Davis is adept at suggesting a world beyond the fewest words, in a way that implies character and conflict.

There is a sense in which Davis's fondness for ultra-short stories reflects her status as a postmodernist. This is so partly because the issue of authenticity can be seen to be part of the aesthetic of smallness. For instance, Davis herself has said that to write too much about a subject can be to distort it, and for this reason she has championed the fragment as a form of veracity:

> It can be seen as a response to the philosophical problem of seeing the written thing replace the subject of writing. If we catch only a little of our subject, or only badly, clumsily, incoherently, perhaps we have not destroyed it. We have written about it … and allowed it to live on at the same time, allowed it to live on in our ellipses, our silences.[13]

This is in keeping with postmodern scepticism and its suspicion of narrative that seeks to explain everything; by contrast postmodernism tends to favour less ambitious statements. Postmodernists often advocate statements that do not take themselves seriously, such as comic or ironic ones, or fragments that make modest, limited assertions. Davis, it seems, is more likely to trust succinct narratives not to 'destroy' their subjects with absolutist or comprehensive ambitions; for her, 'form is a response to doubt'.

Rather than use the term 'story' to describe Davis's shorter writing, Melora Wolff prefers to call them 'pieces',[14] again because many don't have the same emphasis on narrative shape as conventional stories: they don't always have a discernible plot, or emphasis on action. However we choose to describe them, Davis's strategies as a storyteller always feel appropriate for whatever subject she chooses – in other words, subject and form always seem suited. Responding to this quality, Christopher Ricks writes that he would like to use the word 'devoir' to describe her stories: 'a devoir: one's chosen task, one's duty, the utmost one can do'. ['Introduction', *Collected Stories*, xx] This reflects what appears to be Davis's desire not to be bound by orthodox narrative strategies, but to let instinct rather than convention shape the form: Ricks appears to feel that her commitment to her vocation as a writer dictates her expression, and her form[s] develop out of that compulsion.

9

The Art of the Micro Story: 'The Judgement'

ONE OF THE EFFECTS OF DECREASING the number of words in a narrative, of course, is that it focuses the reader's attention on the words that are actually included. This suits Davis's interest in language, and her fondness for precision. Some of the most interesting examples are texts focusing on the meaning of one word. For instance, consider this single-sentence story, 'Judgement', from the collection *Can't and Won't*:

> Into how small a space the word judgement can be compressed: it must fit inside the brain of a ladybug as she, before my eyes, makes a decision.[15]

Here focus is on the word 'judgment', and the brevity of the story invites the reader to reflect on the meaning of that word: the conciseness of the piece throws the word into relief, but leaves the reader to unpack its meaning in relation to the few details on offer. The idea of a word being compressed in an insect's head is surreal and funny, because ultimately judgement refers to an ability to make decisions, not to entities that have dimensions and which can be compacted. But the real point resides in how we interpret the word, and whether or not it is used accurately in this scene. To what extent is an insect's behaviour governed by judgement, as we might understand it? Do insects make judgements, or do they react instinctively? The more we think about the issues raised by Davis's clever positioning of the word here, the more we are forced to confront the difficult philosophical question of free will. We readers are implicitly implicated in this: is it possible for *us* to claim free will? The narrator imposes the notion of free will on an insect, and we assume it for ourselves, but while it seems legitimate to do so in our own case, is it *really*?

'Judgement' is an exquisite miniature perfectly illustrating how Davis can engage us with the minutia of language and meaning in her stories. The title, 'Judgement', is well chosen here, because it adds substance to a scene that wouldn't otherwise bear the weight of our attention: it gives us an indication of how we should interpret it. And of course, the very short length is apposite to the theme, crucial in focusing us on the important word, and the philosophical reflections it generates.

10

The Art of the Micro Story: *Can't and Won't*

JUDGEMENT OF A DIFFERENT KIND PROVIDES the theme of the title story of Davis's collection, *Can't and Won't*, quoted here in full:

> I was recently denied a writing prize because, they said, I was *lazy*. What they meant by lazy was that I used too many contractions: for instance, I would not write out in full the words *cannot* and *will not*, but instead contracted them to *can't* and *won't*. [*Collected Stories*, 46]

The brevity of this story once more complements the subject, given that it is actually about the contraction of phrases. The absurdity of the judges' verdict is easy to see, particularly when we remember that narrative economy is generally praised in writing, hence the cliché, 'less is more'. So one question this story raises is: in what sense can such judges be seen as fit to evaluate art if they consider shortness akin to laziness? Are, say, writers of haiku also to be condemned as lazy, or inferior to writers who produce longer works? In what sense would it be right to call a haiku writer like Matsuo Bashō inferior to Edmund Spenser, author of *The Faerie Queene*, one of the longest poems in English. What about a minimalist composer such as John Cage – is his 1952 piece 433 , where music is entirely absent, inferior to Wagner's Ring Cycle, which plays for roughly fifteen hours? Again, what at first glance appears a simple, even trivial story, creates significant questions that invite reflection and debate.

Presumably we are meant to see the title of the story as an indication that the speaker 'can't' or 'won't' be changing her style to please judges of writing competitions any time soon!

11

The Art of the Micro Story: 'The Old Vacuum Cleaner Keeps Dying on Her'

AT THE CLOSE OF MANY OF DAVIS'S shortest stories, we have the impression that the narrative has been momentarily suspended, rather than terminated. Melora Wolff, for instance, argues that they 'do not end so much as stop: we often have the distinct sense that the speaker or narrator has merely paused for breath, or has been "temporarily interrupted". ['Eye of the Storm', 160] One nice comic example of this effect is 'The Old Vacuum Cleaner Keeps Dying on Her', quoted here in full:

> The old vacuum cleaner keeps dying on her
> over and over
> until at last the cleaning woman
> scares it by yelling
> 'Motherfucker!' [*Can't and Won't*, 226]

There is humour in the impression that the cleaning woman is being mocked by this vacuum cleaner, and it is almost as if the vacuum might actually be responding to her shouts: she 'scares' it into action. The cyclic, interminable nature of the experience suggested by 'over and over' implies that she is trapped, of course, and this darkens the tone a little. What is particularly interesting is how the sense of continuing conflict reflects something that most people can identify with, addressing a common human experience: we not only recognise the woman's annoyance, but we also identify with her irrational response. The tension is not resolved at the close, but continues with the image of the cleaning woman's perpetual frustration. The best miniature fictions are those that remain open in this way: closed or pat endings can make such small narratives seem trite, or joke-like. Davis is extremely adept at avoiding this problem: her miniature work picks up on and articulates the enduring conflicts that inform all of our lives, rarely, if ever, offering resolution.

12

The Art of the Micro Story: 'Away from Home'

DAVIS IS ALSO SKILFUL AT IMPLYING a sense of character in her micro fictions. Even the shortest have a human dimension, and suggest character conflict of some kind. Consider, for instance, the following ten-word piece, 'Away from Home':

> It has been so long since she used a metaphor. [*Collected Stories*, 467]

As with the story, 'Judgement', above, and as so often in micro fictions generally, the title of the story gives us an indication of how we should read it, providing a context of interpretation for the lines that follow. It implies that the unnamed protagonist hasn't made use of metaphor since she has been away from home. But what can this mean? Perhaps it links the use of metaphor to being at home, and the absence of metaphor to travel. We can only speculate about why this might be the case of course, but, again, the extreme brevity of the piece forces us to focus on the key terms: metaphor, and home. As we speculate about their meaning in relation to the protagonist, our sense of her as a character inevitably deepens. She is perhaps someone who becomes more literal when she moves away from home, for instance: is she less likely to make use of implicit comparisons or substitutions when she is away from home? Maybe she is able to appreciate similarities and associations more readily when she is at home? Might this have something to do with the fact that, when she is away from home, she converses with people in languages other than her own, where metaphors might be misunderstood? Perhaps it is only when grounded in the familiar that she can transfer meaning from one thing to another with confidence? Perhaps, in this sense, the story is meant to suggest something about the effects of deracination or dislocation: in other words it might hint at the psychological or emotional consequences of being away from home? Does she need metaphor when she is at home as opposed to when she is away? If so, why? Certainly it forces us to think about what a metaphor is and why it might be employed. Perhaps not least, it invites us to speculate about what kind of character would recognise a lack of metaphorical constructions in her discourse anyway. A translator maybe?

13

Identity, and the Instability of the Self: 'In a House Besieged'

DAVIS'S STORIES ARE OFTEN ABOUT UNSTABLE characters who yearn to be grounded in the world. As we have seen, both of the central characters in 'Story' and 'Orlando' are like this: unsettled and destabilised by their lack of certainty. Many Davis characters lack stability as a result of doubt, and are crippled by indecision. To use Melora Wolff's words, her characters often exhibit a 'perpetual instability of the self'. ['Eye of the Storm', 162] An excellent example is the early story, 'In a House Besieged', quoted here in full.

> In a house besieged lived a man and a woman. From where they cowered in the kitchen the man and woman heard small explosions. 'The wind,' said the woman. 'Hunters,' said the man. 'The rain,' said the woman. 'The army,' said the man. The woman wanted to go home, but she was already home, there in the middle of the country in a

house besieged. [*Collected Stories*, 66]

The couple in this story are incompatible, and that is revealed through their differing responses to the besieged house. The 'explosions' that she perceives as 'wind', for instance, he perceives as 'hunters'; what she interprets as 'rain', he interprets as the 'army'. In other words, she seeks more positive terms than he does: while she strives to make the noises safe, he does the opposite. Her need to view them as harmless is disrupted by her husband's alternative interpretations, and the story illustrates the dislocation between words and the world, signifiers and the signified. Her chosen signifiers, 'wind' and 'rain' cannot be fixed to the unknown noises, and of course signifiers can never be fixed because the world will always remain beyond our attempts to contain it in language. This fact becomes specific to her in the final line when she is made aware of the distinction between a 'house' and a 'home'. Trying to call her house a home is as futile as her other definitions: its status as a hostile 'house besieged' won't be transformed by the application of the word 'home', despite how much she might want it to be. The world simply won't conform to our definitions. The instability of language parallels the woman's own instability – her sense of homelessness. Her predicament doesn't end with the final line, of course, because it is one that can have no end, such is the nature of language, and such is the inevitable 'instability of the self' that relies on language for its mooring. Once more a powerful sense of the character's unresolved conflicts persists, and this is partly what gives the piece force, the feeling of perpetual tension resonating beyond the close of the narrative. As readers, we carry our engagement with her character's plight away with us.

See how the brevity of the story is perfectly suited to the theme here again: the shorter the story, the more the reader is forced to focus on the key words, and the more we are compelled to share the woman's appreciation of their instability. Where in longer narratives the significance of individual words might be attenuated by the extended context, brevity throws it into relief; here it reveals the fluidity and ambiguity of language and invites us to dwell on this.

14

Identity, and the Instability of the Self: 'What She Knew'

ANOTHER EARLY MICRO STORY, 'WHAT SHE Knew', addresses the 'perpetual instability of the self' more directly. Again I include it here in full:

> People did not know what she knew, that she was not really a woman but a man, often a fat man, but more often, probably, an old man. The fact that she was an old man made it hard for her to be a young woman. It was hard for her to talk to a young man, for instance, though the young man was clearly interested in her. She had to ask herself, Why is this young man flirting with this old man? [*Collected Stories*, 32]

The alternative identities that the central character constructs for herself here all seem unstable: neither her gender, her size, nor her age are constant. However, because she cannot literally undergo these shifts in age, size, and gender, we assume she thinks in terms of metaphor, which again highlights the status of words as unstable comparisons, as opposed to fixed descriptors. So, *metaphorically speaking* she can be a man, perhaps old, often fat. But this could mean so many different things, because the word man, and the concept of male, together with words like old and fat, have so many different potential implications. The instability and uncertainty is highlighted by the use of terms such as 'often' and 'probably', and again the story seems to reflect Davis's reluctance to give credence to the notion of a stable self. It is possible to be a young woman, and yet still be described as a man, old and fat: the nature of language and metaphor allow that flexibility, as does the nature of identity. One can be a woman and feel like a man, for instance; one can identify with men rather than women, and so on. Identity, like language, is fluid.

Once more the brevity gives key words a profile that may be overlooked or diminished in a longer narrative. The story has a limited context which augments the potential for ambiguity: the confinement ensures that the ambivalent nature of the important words becomes a focus for our attention, highlighting the identity crisis on which the story hangs. The force of the piece is dependent on the ambiguity that the restricted context helps create, and again there is a sense that this conflict will not end with the close of the story. It constructs identity as an enigma, and we are left with the impression that the character will have to live with her awareness of this, even as it undermines her sense of a stable self, and her ability to relate to others.

15

Lydia Davis and Humour

ONE REVIEWER NOTED THAT LYDIA DAVIS, 'displays a deadpan humour', in much of her writing, comparing her 'delight in stealthy jokes' to the work of the American writer Donald Barthelme, and, before him, Franz Kafka.[16] This is an apt comparison that many others have made. Like Davis, Kafka and Barthelme both had an interest in the short form, and used it as a vehicle for a distinctive humour born, particularly in Kafka's case, of his often disengaged, straight-faced representation of the absurd. As with Kafka, Davis's characters frequently find themselves in ludicrous situations, often of their own making, and while this becomes increasingly funny for the reader, laughter offers no respite for characters trapped in a comic snare that is both humorous and nightmarish. The comedy is augmented by the fact that these situations are narrated in a detached, matter-of-fact way that never acknowledges either the absurdity of the situation, or its potential for humour. In Kafka's work we see humour in the lengths the characters go to in order to try to establish themselves in their world, or indeed to even understand it. Josef K. in *The Trial*, for instance, is accused of a crime on the first page, and spends the rest of the story trying to discover the precise details of the accusation made against him. It becomes his obsession, but as the story develops we get the impression that this obsession actually comes from within Josef K. himself, and he could simply ignore his accusers and live contentedly if he chose. As he struggles to make sense of his life we also begin to see that the struggle is actually all there is to his existence. As the late American writer David Foster Wallace points out, central to Kafka's humour is the sense that:

> The horrific struggle to establish a human self results in a self whose humanity is inseparable from that horrific struggle. That our endless and impossible journey toward home is in fact our home.[17]

We saw a similar fixation in the central character of 'Story', where the character obsesses over an elusive truth, and in the relentless paranoia of Mrs Orlando. As with Kafka's heroes, their attempt to interpret life, or to impose some sense of meaning on it, *is* their life. That stasis, and lack of insight into their predicament, is characteristic of both Davis and Kafka. The humour is derived partly from our sense of superiority over these individuals, but also partly from our identification with their feelings of frustration and entrapment. While we can sometimes empathise with, and feel sympathy for, these characters, it's not always easy because, as I say, we feel they are partly to blame for their own distress. Sometimes, for instance, they appear to be caught in the snare of their own apathy, as in the following Davis micro fiction, quoted in full:

> 'In the Garment District'
> A man has been making deliveries in the garment district for years now: every morning he takes the same garments on a moving rack through the streets to a shop and every evening takes them back again to the warehouse. This happens because there is a dispute between the shop and the warehouse which cannot be settled: the shop denies it ever ordered the clothes, which are badly made and of cheap material and by now years out of style; while the warehouse will not take responsibility because the clothes cannot be returned to the wholesalers, who have no use for them. To the man all this is nothing. They are not his clothes, he is paid for this work, and he intends to leave the company soon, though the right moment has not yet come. [*Collected Stories*, 200]

There is humour in the ridiculousness of the situation – we can laugh, for instance, at the childishness of the dispute between the shop and the warehouse. We laugh at the central character too perhaps: while the man appears to have some insight into his situation, and does not search for meaning in the manner of other Davis heroes, he is still trapped, this time by apathy and his aversion to finding a more meaningful job. We are told that he has been doing this job 'for years now', and, though he ostensibly plans to leave, the implication of the phrase, 'the right moment has not yet come' is that nothing will change. In this way the piece could be seen as a comment on the very human tendency to procrastinate; or, from a political perspective, it could be making a general point about the futility of life within capitalism. His job is meaningless and dehumanising, but the worker's readiness to be reconciled to this perpetuates the status quo. We may moan about our unfulfilling jobs, but as long as they provide for us economically, the revolution will be a long time coming. Certainly this wry comment on the human condition has a very Kafkaesque feel.

16

Lydia Davis and Puns

WE HAVE SEEN THAT DAVIS IS profoundly interested in language, and the playful way she explores it is also very often a source of humour. In one of her best-known miniature stories, 'A Mown Lawn', she takes her examination of the phrase 'mown lawn' to comical extremes. The story is quoted here in full:

> She hated a *mown lawn*. Maybe that was because *mow* was the reverse of *wom*, the beginning of the name of what she was – a *woman*. A *mown lawn* had a sad sound to it, like a *long moan*. From her, a *mown lawn* made a *long moan*. *Lawn* had some of the letters of *man*, though the reverse of *man* would be *Nam*, a bad war. A *raw war*. *Lawn* also contained the letters of *law*. In fact, *lawn* was a contraction of *lawman*. Certainly a *lawman* could and did *mow a lawn*. *Law and order* could be seen as starting from *lawn order*, valued by so many Americans. *More lawn* could be made using a *lawn mower*. A *lawn mower* did make *more lawn*. *More lawn* was a contraction of *more lawmen*. Did *more*

lawn in America make *more lawmen* in America? Did *more lawn* make *more Nam? More mown lawn* made *more long moan*, from her. Or a *lawn mourn*. So often, she said, Americans wanted *more mown lawn*. All of America might be one *long mown lawn*. A *lawn* not *mown* grows *long*, she said: better a *long lawn*. Better a *long lawn* and a *mole*. Let the *lawman* have the *mown lawn*, she said. Or the *moron*, the *lawn moron*. [*Collected Stories*, 314]

There is comedy in the obsessive tone of the narrator here, but the humour mainly derives from the exaggerated puns. Most people would think it unlikely that a mown lawn could cause discomfort because of its affinities with the Vietnam War! At first sight such connections seem tenuous, and indeed the product of a comically compulsive mind. The repetitions underscore this notion, and this is particularly evident when the piece is read aloud: it is hard to read this aloud or listen to it read without laughing. But of course after a moment's reflection we can see that this is how language works – all words have connotations far beyond the dictionary definitions, and these are often very specific to the individual, based on personal experiences with particular words, and also based on how words sound. Words can never be considered in isolation – the fact that 'mown' is a homophonic pun of 'moan', always has the potential to affect the way we relate to it. Again, then, Davis makes the point that the meaning of words can't be pinned down; you would have to be a 'moron' to think otherwise!

In some ways this is a subversive piece that appears to

be criticising conformity – the people who worry about mown lawns are people who adhere too readily to the dictates of the powers that be, perhaps, suggesting that these advocates of 'law and order' don't always have our best interests at heart (they can be inclined to take us in to 'bad' wars if we are not careful). Law, like language, tends to be a slippery thing too, dependent on context and interpretation, and this piece comically reminds us of that fact. So while we might laugh at the hyperbole and repetition, we also respect its subversive dimension and its willingness to challenge the authority of meaning.

17

The Process of Writing and 'The Center of the Story'

MANY OF DAVIS'S STORIES ARE ABOUT the act of storytelling itself – her stories are often self-conscious in that they comment on their own processes. Traditional fiction doesn't do this, of course – it strives to convince us that it is offering a window on reality and does its best to make us forget that we are reading fiction. When stories draw attention to their fictional status they are sometimes called metafictions – they are, in a sense, fictions that don't pretend to be anything other than fictional: they admit their constructedness and artificiality.

One excellent example of a metafiction is Davis's 'The Center of the Story', which appeared in the collection, *Almost No Memory* (1997). It is about an author who is dissatisfied with a story because she cannot determine what the story is about – in other words she cannot decide where the centre of her story lies. The narrator lists some of the things the story has in it – it features a hurricane (albeit one that only threatens to strike), and religion, although the author doesn't really want it to be about religion because 'religion was not something she wanted to write about'. [*Collected Stories*, 173] As we read it becomes evident that the author has been involved in similar events to those she is trying to write about in her story. We are told, for instance, that 'She was reading the Bible in a time of hurricane'. [173] The narrator also tells us that 'She [the author] had started the story with her landlady, an old lady from Trinidad … thinking of writing a letter to the president'. [174] We don't know whether this refers to the author's 'real' landlady (the one she has in real life), but we are told that 'She [the author] will probably take out the president and the landlady, but leave in the Bible and the hurricane'. [174] The author thinks that if she can strip down the story – edit out the superfluities – then the centre of the story, and hence the meaning, might revel itself. Also in her story there is a man who thinks that he is dying, even though he is only suffering from food poisoning. He is shown lying on his bed feeling poorly at the time when the hurricane is about to strike. The narrator tells us that 'it is unclear what his place is, in the story', except that he is uncertain about religion and God. Again it seems as if the man has had some kind of relationship with Davis's fictional author, and hence she is trying to rework something from her life into fiction. Davis's author is a woman who at one time in her life used to visit churches and synagogues, and, despite the fact that she is not a 'believer', she has 'an unusual, religious sort of peace in her.' The narrator also tells us that in researching her story the author has been reading the Bible, and is beginning to wonder if the story might be about this sense of peace she feels. Perhaps this is the centre of the story, then, a sense of peace that allows 'her to accept the possibility of the worst sort of disaster, one even worse than a hurricane'? [176] As we read we are meant to feel that the process of the author writing the story is ongoing, and we are witnessing her struggling to find its centre. By the time we reach the 'end of the story as it is now', the author still has the problem of its missing centre. At this point she begins to wonder if 'there may be no centre'; or if perhaps,

> there is a centre but the centre is empty, either because she has not yet found what belongs there, or because it is meant to be empty: there, but empty, the in the same way that the man is sick but not dying, the hurricane approached but did not strike, and she had a religious calm, but no faith. [177]

Thus the story is about an author's (possibly Davis's own?) attempts to establish what her story is about, and the process of enquiry and reflection *is* the story. It implies that meaning – the centre of the story – is not something that exists independently of the story, or that precedes the story, it is something that is created *in* or *by* the story, once the author has determined where the centre of the story lies.

The centre (the meaning of the story) is made (constructed) in this sense. Perhaps this what she means by the centre being empty. In a manner of speaking, emptiness seems to be the point here, and all stories are empty in this respect: they have no meaning other than the meanings we create *for* them as we struggle to find their centres as writers, or indeed as readers: clearly it stresses that centres are not fixed – they are about judgement and consensus; there is nothing in any story that can tell you finally and definitively what it is about; so where can the centre of any story lie?

The elusiveness of the centre is not necessarily the same as meaninglessness. Davis's author's story contains a hurricane that doesn't strike, but this hurricane still has an effect on the characters in her story, so much so that its threat alone is enough to create a story! Similarly, with the man who is sick rather than dying, surely the significant thing as far as he is concerned is that he *believes* he is dying: that belief may be based on a fiction, but it still has profound significance to him. Likewise, Davis's author doesn't have religious faith (she doesn't believe that religious stories are *literally* true), but literal truth isn't necessary for those religious stories to affect her in positive ways: she has her 'religious sort of peace', after all. In other words, all of these stories are potentially empty, but all are potentially significant if that significance can be found, constructed, in a way that makes sense to the author and her readers. In this respect it is writers and readers who are at the centre of this, and all stories.

18

The Process of Writing and 'What Was Interesting'

PUBLISHED IN THE SAME 1997 COLLECTION is another metafiction, 'What Was Interesting', which has a similar metafictional feel. It opens with the line, 'It was hard for her to write this story, too, or rather she should say it is hard for her to write it well'. [*Collected Stories*, 204] The 'too' implies that we are meant to see this author ('She') as the same author who struggled to find a centre in the previous story. Here she is struggling after showing a work in progress to a friend who criticised it for being boring. The author's story is about an argument she had with her boyfriend (so again it has some basis in her 'real' life). She had been hoping to spend an evening discussing travel plans with him, but he ended their date prematurely when he unceremoniously put her in to a cab with two other men, instructing her to go home. This had made her angry, but her friend feels that the incident in itself isn't interesting enough to sustain her story. So 'What Was Interesting' narrates the author's reflections on this, and about how she might best communicate her anger to the reader, and hence make it more viable as 'interesting' fiction.

We are told about the author's evening after she arrives home in the cab: she spends time crying, before deciding to go to a friend's empty apartment to spend the night sleeping 'on his living room rug'. The following morning she returns to her own apartment, maintaining that 'She would never disclose this to her friend, even though disclosing it would make for an interesting aspect of the story'. Indeed, we are told that 'this friend would possibly have been the most interesting person in the story, if she had put him instead of his apartment into it'. [209] The question a reader might ask at this point, of course, is: why didn't she do exactly that? Why not include the friend if this would make for a more interesting story? Is it because this has no basis in reality, and she is squeamish about including something in her story that didn't actually happen? Does she need to adhere to the facts of her life rather than make things up? She doesn't say so, but the fact that she alludes to this potentially more interesting story implies it, and perhaps this is designed to augment our sense of the authenticity of what she *does* choose to tell us? In other words, it seems as if the author wants to make a lived experience interesting, without distorting it. This raises important points about why we read and write fiction. We want stories to be entertaining, but we also want them to feel authentic. But shouldn't the truth be more interesting than fiction? It seems to be for Davis's author, but not for the man to whom she showed the story. However, in the broader sense, the story of her attempts to make her story interesting *is* interesting, this *does* feel authentic, and ultimately *this* is what engages us in the story.

In the closing paragraph we are told that, the day following the argument, the author was sick from drinking too much the night before. However, she felt that it would be 'more interesting' in her story if she was well rather than sick after drinking heavily; but she preferred to be sick, we are told, because being sick felt like a 'celebration of the change that had happened' between her and her boyfriend. So presumably this is an example of an author ignoring what a reader might find interesting, focusing instead on what has relevance to her own emotions. Of course by this stage the distinction between what actually happened in the author's life, and what is represented via the *narrator's* account of *her* account of it, is rather hard to untangle! The distinction between truth and fiction is blurred. And as is often the case, we cannot help but wonder what relevance this might have to the 'real' author's (Davis's) life, which adds another layer of complication to the story.

Ultimately the author concludes that, while her friend doesn't feel that her anger is interesting enough, this anger is certainly the interesting thing *for her*: 'this anger of hers, lasting so long, was certainly more interesting to her, because in the end she found it harder to explain than the fact that she had loved him so long'. [209] As suggested, however, what draws the reader through the story is the author's reflections on which aspects of it should be conveyed, and what force they might have for the reader. All stories are about characters with problems, but this character's problem isn't the fact that she has been hurt by her boyfriend; rather it concerns how she might turn that into art, how she might use and understand her anger as a writer. Her anger is only interesting to her, but the problem she has representing it in art it is undoubtedly interesting to us.

19

Lydia Davis and Reading: 'The Letter'

WE HAVE SEEN DAVIS'S INTEREST IN the making of art, but some of her stories also address the issue of how to interpret it. One of the first to explore this is 'The Letter', from the collection *Break it Down*, about a woman who receives a letter from her ex-lover. The relationship between the two is similar to that presented in 'Story', where the woman obsesses about the implications of her lover's actions. The protagonist here is also obsessive, and again this is taken to comic extremes in the story. We are told, for instance, that: 'she cannot say to herself that it is really over, even though [...] he has moved to another city, hasn't been in touch for more than a year, and is married to another woman'. [*Collected Stories*, 40] When they parted he had told her, cryptically, 'Maybe in ten years', and she had answered, 'Maybe in five, but he didn't answer that'. [42] The open-ended parting left the possibility of reconciliation alive in her mind, and she is excited when she receives a letter from him. It takes the form of a poem written in French, but not composed by him. He has copied it out by hand, and while receiving it initially makes her feel happy, she later feels sick and angry when she discovers its cryptic nature. Much of the story is devoted to the woman's attempts to interpret the poem (which of course she must translate into English), and assess its meaning and implications. She begins with the postmark on the envelope, the date, the manner in which he has handwritten her address, how he has formed the letters in his words, all for clues about the circumstances of the letter's composition, and its inferences: 'He must have mailed this somewhere out of his neighbourhood,' she says at one point, 'Did he also write it away from home? Where?' Again, then, the obsessive dimension of her character is made clear. As she reads the poem, some words are difficult to decipher due to the handwriting, and even when she feels she has established what the words on the page are, they are laden with ambiguity. At first she interprets the poem as suggesting the two of them might get back together again: 'There seems to be no doubt [...] that he is still thinking, eight hundred miles from here, that it will be possible ten years from now, or five years, or, since a year has already passed, nine years or four years from now'. [45] Notice how effectively Davis comically underscores her character's fixation, with her reference to the time that has already elapsed: she is counting down the years toward her improbable dream in a way that makes her seem deluded, but also touchingly human. Given the poem's ambiguity, it is also open to negative readings, and of course she cannot help but entertain these too: we are told that, 'she worries about the dying part of [the poem]: it could mean that he does not really expect to see her again [...] or that time will be so long it will be a lifetime'. [45] Or perhaps the poem – whatever it might mean – is not what her ex-lover is thinking at all, just the closest thing to what he was thinking; in other words, even if she deciphers the handwriting correctly, then gets the translation of the words right, then gets the *interpretation* of the words right, she still has no guarantee that it meant to him what it means to her. The story ends with her smelling the letter, because she thinks she can smell her old lover on it. She smells the paper, and then the poem: 'and she thinks she can smell something there, though she is probably smelling only the ink'. [46]

This is a story about how the onus of interpretation is always on the reader, and how reading is a creative activity in itself, and never clear cut. Like the metafictions discussed above, it is partly about the construction of meaning – how we make meanings that are never absolute or final, and which can never be said to constitute the truth. Ambiguity is always pervasive, and we can make more than one meaning out of almost anything. The final reference to her smelling the ink and thinking she can detect something there is itself ambiguous. That ambiguity is suggested by the words, 'she is probably smelling only the ink'; 'probably' speaks of possibilities rather than certainties, and that is all we can ever do as readers.

20

Lydia Davis and Reading: 'Foucault and the Pencil'

A STORY DEALING WITH A SIMILAR issue is 'Foucault and the Pencil', from the collection, *Almost No Memory*. This is about a woman in the process of translating a piece of writing by the French philosopher Michel Foucault (1926-1984). At the same time as translating we see her intermittently make notes in a notebook. Indeed the story itself is written in a clipped, notational style. At first she is in a counsellor's waiting room, ahead of an appointment; during her meeting with the counsellor she apparently discusses a 'conflict' that has been causing her concern and creating arguments between her and an unnamed other. On leaving she takes the subway and tries to resume her translation project, but the argument she has just been discussing distracts her. We learn that the argument was about travel, and she begins to think about how the 'argument itself became a form of travel, each sentence carrying arguers on to next sentence, next sentence on to next, and in the end, arguers were not where they had started'. [*Collected Stories*, 151] Eventually she stops thinking about the argument and tries to refocus on Foucault, although she finds him hard to understand. She stops, makes a note in her notebook about her fellow passengers, then returns to her thoughts about the argument. It strikes her that the argument isn't only like a travelling vehicle, but also like a plant or hedge, with the hedge growing to obscure light. She makes another note in her notebook – a question that she intends to ask about the argument – then returns again to Foucault. As she works on the translation she begins to notice the places in the text where Foucault is harder to understand than others. She makes a note about these in her notebook, considering it progress because, 'now at least understood lack of understanding reading Foucault'. [153] The story ends with her thinking again about the argument, and making another note about it in her notebook: 'made note of same question about argument as before though with stress on a different word'. [153] So now it seems as if she understands more about the nature of the problem, if not how to resolve it. Reading Foucault has helped her deepen her understanding of the problem: the act of analysing where her difficulties lay in translating Foucault, have impacted on this problem she is having in her life – the problem still remains, but possibly reframed in a way that might be helpful. Again the story deals with the elusive nature of meaning – here this is illustrated via the parallel Davis draws between her character's argument, and the act of translation. When analysing the argument she realises that it is like a vehicle, with one sentence leading to another, just seeming to extend rather than resolve the argument. Language is exactly like that, with meaning infinitely deferred along a never ending chain of signifiers. Thus if you search for a definition of a word, that definition merely leads to another definition, and so on. It is a 'form of travel' that never arrives at a destination – a single meaning. The protagonist wants to resolve her conflict, which is why she is seeing a counsellor, but the implication is that she will only ever achieve a reframing of that conflict – perhaps another perspective on it that she had previously missed. While this might not constitute a solution, it does have the potential to move one forward; and to reach an understanding of one's 'lack of understanding' is a significant achievement in itself.

21

Lydia Davis and Intertextuality: 'Southward Bound, Reads *Worstward Ho*'

ANOTHER ASPECT OF DAVIS'S SELF CONSCIOUSNESS has to do with intertextuality – in other words, the ways in which her texts make use of other texts. Writers never write in isolation, and most texts contain allusions to other texts; indeed, most texts – probably all texts – are to some degree dependent on the texts that precede them insofar as they employ plots, styles, themes, tropes, figures of speech, and characters that have been used in the myriad of texts that have already been written. Some writers, particularly experimental and postmodern writers, like to make an issue of this by being explicit about it; they draw attention to their dependence on the already written, overtly signalling their intertextuality. Certainly many of Davis's stories have interesting relationships with the already written. One example is 'Southward Bound, Reads

Worstward Ho', a piece that appeared in the 2007 collection, *Varieties of Disturbance*. It concerns a woman on a journey south, reading Samuel Beckett's novella, *Worstward Ho* (1983). It offers an account of the journey in a style that is a pastiche of Beckett's style, copying the clipped, elliptical prose that he employs in that novella. The story opens with the following paragraph: 'Sun in eyes, faces east, waits for van bound for south meeting plane from west. Carries book, *Worstword H.*'. [*Collected Stories*, 571] However, she accompanies this primary narrative with a series of footnotes that complement the story, adding substance to the narrative in a style that is more detailed and expansive. So the first footnote develops the first paragraph thus,

> She waits near the highway before the entrance of Hojo's for the van going south to meet a plane coming from the west – waiting with her is a thin dark haired woman who does not stop walking back and forth relentlessly near her luggage […] In her purse she has two books, *Worstward Ho*, and *West with the Night*. If it is quiet and she reads *Worstward Ho* on the way south, when she is fresh, she can read *West with the Night* on the way back up north, when it will be later and she will be tired. [571]

You can see how the footnote adds to the primary narrative, developing the context, and unpacking the character's actions and thoughts. Indeed in terms of word length, the footnotes occupy more of the story than the primary narrative. The story quotes directly from Beckett's novella as she reads it, both in the primary narrative and in the footnotes – she uses quotation marks to denote Beckett's words in the latter, but not in the former where Davis lets Beckett's narrative merge with her narrator's. Throughout the course of the story Davis's character manages to finish *Worstward Ho*, but feels a little ambivalent towards it, liking some sections, but not others.

This Davis story is a highly experimental one which works as literary criticism as well as fiction, presenting a critical commentary on another text, whilst at the same time using that text for its own creative ends. As Jonathan Evans suggests, 'It can be viewed as a homage [to Beckett], although the criticisms [...] suggest that this homage is not unequivocal'. [*Many Voices*, 137] An important aspect of the story is that it is hard to read it without reflecting on the relevance of the source text to our interpretation of Davis's story. Not surprisingly, some critics have seen it as a comment of Beckett's aesthetic, and on his preoccupations as a writer. As Nathan Ihara says:

> Reading a difficult story about a person having difficulty reading a difficult story is exasperating, even outraging. Of course, this kind of frustration is exactly what Beckett's story is about. *Worstward Ho* is an existential lament over the unending frustrations of life, a Sisyphean howl. The woman in the van, with her constant attempts and failures to read and understand Beckett's text, embodies Beckett's basic dilemma, but in a hilariously mundane fashion.[18]

At the very least this story feeds off the original in an interesting way, making Beckett's themes its own to some degree. It would certainly be hard to make sense of the story without at least some knowledge of the novella she references. Many stories of this type also remind us of the elusive nature of originality. Where do stories originate, given their dependence on the already written? This question is underscored by the fact that the Beckett story also signals a pre-existing text: his title, *Worstward Ho*, alludes to the 1855 novel *Westwood Ho!*, by Charles Kingsley. The point is that stories tend to be underlain by infinite substrata of pre-existing stories; and origins, like meanings, remain beyond our grasp.

22

Lydia Davis and Intertextuality: 'Kafka Comes to Dinner'

ANOTHER STORY THAT INVOKES THE THEMES and aesthetic of another writer is, 'Kafka Comes to Dinner', again from *Varieties of Disturbance*. This story imagines Franz Kafka preparing to cook a romantic meal for a lady called Milena (who in real life was Kafka's Czech translator). Davis tells how her story includes 'reworked quotations from [Kafka's own] *Letters to Milena*', [quoted in Evans, *Many Voices,* 134], and, as Jonathan Evans notes, the whole piece copies Kafka's style, and the 'doom-laden tone' of his most famous stories. [134] The story has the feel of parody, as if it is sending Kafka up by comically exaggerating both his style, and the behaviour that characterises his heroes. Kafka spends the duration of the story worrying about the forthcoming meal, and his anxiety is expressed in hyperbolic terms which seem ludicrously incongruous given the circumstances. After inviting Melina to dinner, for instance, Kafka initially tells us that he is 'at peace'; but 'Then I began to torment myself, like a flower in a flower box that is thrashed by the wind but loses not a single petal'. [*Collected Stories*, 511] Like a typical Kafka hero he is ensnared by his anxiety, although given the benign circumstances of his predicament, this anxiety seems hugely disproportionate, and elicits humour as opposed to menace and dread. It is typical of Davis that she should exploit this kind of angst for humour – Kafka here seems as ridiculous as some of her own heroes, who, as we have seen, also appear to obsess over trivial things. As with the previous story, this again depends on the reader having some knowledge of Kafka and his work. While we might still see humour in the over-the-top fretting of the hero, our appreciation is augmented when we read it in the light of Kafka's own stories. In some respects the story has a debunking feel to it, which adds force to the humour, but it also offers a worthwhile insight into Kafka himself. There is a sense in which many of Kafka's heroes are also *meant* to be seen as ridiculous: as suggested above, the point of such novels as *The Trial* is that the hero's problems can be seen as self-imposed. Kafka's own work sometimes seems funny because the hero's guilt appears irrational – Davis picks up on this comic aspect of Kafka and makes it more explicit through parody.

23

Lydia Davis, Intertextuality and Translation: 'The Walk'

WE HAVE SEEN HOW DAVIS REWORKS preexisting material into her stories, using verbatim passages from Beckett in 'Southward Bound', and phrases from Kafka's letters in 'Kafka Cooks Dinner', but she experiments with intertextuality in other ways too. She has translated numerous texts throughout her career, of course, and has occasionally incorporated translated material into her creative writing work. Her story 'The Walk', for instance, incorporates translations of Proust into the narrative: one passage of *Swann's Way* translated by Davis herself, alongside another passage translated by C.K. Scott Moncrieff, whose translation of *Swann's Way* preceded Davis's. The story is about a translator and a critic who are both in Oxford for a conference about translation. The translator (who appears to be a fictional incarnation of Davis herself) has translated Proust, but the critic prefers an earlier version of the same text (the Moncrieff version). Despite their scholarly differences they take an evening stroll together around Oxford, losing their way a little until they happen on a spot that they recognise. The experience reminds the translator of a scene in Proust where Marcel is out walking with his parents. The scene from Proust is then reproduced in both translations, Moncrieff's and Davis's. The two Proust translations about walking implicitly complement and comment on the primary narrative – the account of the walk that the characters are taking – in a way that produces a story about how the present reworks the past, as Siddhartha Deb puts it:

> We have read three passages about circular walks, which may sound indulgent [but] the deceptively simple story becomes a palimpsest in which the current experience is seen to be a rewriting of other, previous experiences, and Proust's memory of a childhood already vanished at the time of its writing comes alive in the evening walk of two middle-aged scholars adrift in a foreign university town.[19]

Davis uses the already written as a foundation for an original piece of work again, then, this time in a piece about the enduring themes of art and their relevance to a specific human encounter. The difference here is that Davis's own work – in the form of her translation of Proust – has been recycled too. It makes a point about how art can be seen to bleed into the lived experience, affecting our judgements and perceptions.

24

Lydia Davis, Intertextuality and Translation: 'Marie Curie, So Honourable a Woman'

DAVIS OFFERS ANOTHER RECYCLING OF A former translation project in her strange story, 'Marie Curie, So Honourable a Woman', from the collection, *Samuel Johnson is Indignant* (2001). This story is effectively a short biography of Marie Curie, written in a deliberately clunky prose style. Its genesis was a full-length biography of Curie, Françoise Giroud's *Une femme honorable* (1981), which she translated as *Marie Curie: A Life* (1986). According to Davis, her translation demanded a particular prose style – a 'cute' prose style to use her words – conventional for such projects. [Davis, quoted in Evans, 112] She became interested in the creative possibilities of this style, deciding to produce a mini version of Giroud's biography using an exaggerated version of it. In Davis's own words: 'this Marie Curie piece is my abbreviated and deliberately awkward and literal translation of excerpts of a real book by a real French author'. [Davis, quoted in Evans, *Many Voices*, 112] When she published the story in book form she did not acknowledge the source, presumably because she wants readers to focus on the story itself – Marie Curie's trajectory as a character and the manner in which it is narrated. This might look like plagiarism to some, but legally it isn't, either in English or U.S. law. The story does not repeat Giroud's text, or Davis's book-length translation of it, verbatim; rather it offers a radically abridged version of the former, in a distinctive style. As a result, while it may be derivative of the source text, it can be considered an original work. [See Evans, 118] Again this story raises interesting questions about originality. Who can be said to have authored this story? Despite the fact that Davis has given Curie's life (or rather Giroud's version of it), a distinctive shape and tone, she certainly cannot claim to have invented it, so in what sense is she the author? And of course Davis makes explicit something that is true of many, perhaps all, stories, regardless of their ostensible relationship to reality, or to other texts: writers do not fully invent *everything* in their work, irrespective of how original it seems; rather they build stories out of material that already exists, such as plots, styles, tropes, and languages that are inherited rather than owned.

25

Lydia Davis, Intertextuality and Translation: Found Stories in Flaubert

ANOTHER, EVEN MORE DIRECT EXAMPLE of Davis creatively reworking translated material is her experiments with Gustave Flaubert's letters. In 2010 Davis published a series of stories in *The Paris Review* titled, 'Ten Stories from Flaubert', later included in the collection *Can't and Won't*. These stories are taken from letters that Flaubert wrote between 1853-4. Here is an example quoted in full.

> 'The Cook's Lesson'
> Today I have learned a great lesson; our cook was my teacher. She is twenty-five years old and she's French. I discovered, when I asked her, that *she did not know* that Louis-Philippe is no longer king of France and we now have a republic. And yet it has been five years since he left the throne. She said the fact that he is no longer king simply does not interest her in the least – those were her words.

And I think of myself as an intelligent man! But compared to her I'm an imbecile. [*Can't and Won't*, 9]

This is a section of one of Flaubert's letters, excerpted and reconceptualised as a story. It works as a stand-alone story because it coheres around a single theme – the mock edification of the speaker – and because of the satirical force of the irony. The cook's ignorance is comically constructed as a sound philosophy of life, not because the narrator believes that it *is* sound, but because it allows him to demonstrate his contempt for both the former king, and the republic. Again Davis did not invent this story – she has merely extracted it from a letter, reframing it as a discrete piece. It is a 'found' story in this sense. You might say that she recognised the potential it had to work on its own terms as a story, so while she didn't invent the story, we must credit her artistic vision. Jonathan Evans says, rightly, that such stories demonstrate 'how the border between [Davis's] persona as a translator and as a writer is porous' [107], and it suggests that when she reads she does so with an eye for potential subjects that might have a life as a story. This is a practice that, as we shall see, extends beyond her reading, to her life in general.

26

Lydia Davis and the Lived Experience: 'St Martin'

As well as drawing on pre-existing texts for material, Davis, like most writers, also makes use of her own life, and the lives of people she knows. She has been doing this throughout her career, drawing on the lived experience in a variety of ways. Some of her writing addresses relationships she has had with men, for instance, and, as she was married to a writer in her early years, it is not surprising that she and Paul Auster occasionally use the same experiences for their art. One example is Davis's story, 'St Martin', which is based on the time the two were paid to housesit in France during the early 1970s. Auster also writes about this in his memoir, 'The Red Notebook'.[20] They both address their financial hardship during this time, focusing on their lack of food, including one anecdote about an onion pie they cooked one day when they were on the brink of starvation. In Auster's version, they begin eating the pie before it was cooked, reluctantly having to return it to the oven even though they desperately wanted to finish it. They go out for a walk, forgetting about the pie, and accidentally let it burn to a point where it became inedible. In Davis's version they return the uncooked pieces to the oven whilst continuing to consume the edible pieces of the pie. The result is identical, but it demonstrates how versions of the same story can differ, and how writers shape them according to their purpose. Auster unpacks this incident in more detail than Davis, who merely mentions it as an aside, or as a supplement to her main theme. She centres her account around the loss of one of the dogs that the two have been asked to look after during their time at the house, something that Auster scarcely mentions. The latter is interested principally in the couple's penury, whilst Davis is much more concerned with the relationship between the two house sitters. It is significant that Auster's 'Notebook' is a memoir, whilst Davis presents her account as a story: it could be said that a short story has certain aesthetic requirements that a memoir does not – readers have expectations about the shape of the narrative and the trajectory of the characters. Readers look for form in short stories; they look for those elements that might suggest purpose and meaning. We have higher expectations because we think of stories in terms of art, and we think of memoir in terms of life. Life is something that 'just happens' whereas we want art to have coherence and significance – if we feel that it doesn't, then we feel cheated. 'St Martin' is a good example of how Davis shapes life to make art; or perhaps another way of putting it, of how she identifies art in life. Consider the opening of the story:

> We were caretakers for most of that year, from early fall until summer. There was a house and grounds to look after, two dogs and two cats. We fed the cats, one white and one calico, who lived outside and ate their meals on the kitchen windowsill, sparring in the sunlight as they waited for their food, but we did not keep the house very clean, or the weeds cut in the yard, and our employers, kind people though they were, probably never quite forgave us for what happened to one of the dogs. [*Collected Stories*, 183]

This is a masterly way to begin a story, creating tension from the outset. From the first paragraph we need to know what exactly happened to the dogs, and this pulls us through the narrative which goes on to detail the lives of the couple and their various struggles to survive. It is not until the end of the story that we find out that one of the dogs disappears when the couple let them out for a run. The references to the dogs at the beginning and end frame the story, giving the incident a degree of significance in relation to the tale as a whole. As with the pie anecdote, it augments our sense of the couple's impracticality – it is *their* fault the dog disappears because they should not have let him run free, and this underscores the notion that the two are bad for one another as a couple. While their relationship is not overtly hostile, it feels potentially destructive, and we cannot help feeling that the loss of the dog augurs the loss of one another. Thus while Davis and Auster both write about this time in their lives, the former sees a plot on which to hang a story. She hasn't invented a plot or fictionalised, as such, but she has selected the necessary details from her experience, and arranged them to create art. She sees a plot in reality. She has spoken about this aspect of her writing in interview:

> real life does have little plots, and it's a lot of fun to take pieces of real life and select from them and then organize them according to a plot. We have plots going on all the time, and all we have to do is isolate them.[21]

This tendency to identify art in her experience is central to her aesthetic, which is very much geared toward manipulation rather than invention.

27

Lydia Davis and the Lived Experience: Found Material

ANOTHER ASPECT OF THIS IMPULSE IS Davis's use of so-called 'found' material from life, which she addresses in a number of interviews. We saw when discussing the Flaubert letter above that 'found' refers to the appropriation or recontextualisation of existing material: in other words, a writer spots something which has an aesthetic appeal that others overlook, and by presenting it as art gives it another dimension. Dana Goodyear offers an example of this happening with an email that Davis received via her university staff account. The original email read:

> Round, faux tortoiseshell glasses, bifocal lenses, lost sometime Friday, between the Nursery School, B Village, A Sacred Space. It would be great if somebody has found them and they aren't in a place covered in a foot of snow!

Davis reworks this email into the following story:

> Personal Announcement
>
> Woman named Shrubbs
> Has lost faux tortoiseshell eyeglasses
>
> Where?
> Somewhere between nursery school
> and sacred place
>
> They are possibly
> covered by snow. [Quoted in Goodyear, 'Long Story Short']

Davis restructures the original to emphasise the elements that she finds interesting. An email request for assistance becomes a poetic short piece that alludes to the journey between childhood and death ('nursery school/and sacred place'), and hints at how a character might find it hard to navigate her way through life. The image of eyeglasses covered in snow is wonderfully evocative, suggestive of our thwarted desire to locate ourselves in the world, and see it for what it is.

Again, Davis didn't invent this story as such, but saw the potential in a text that already existed, and set about teasing out that potential. It is obvious that some texts will need more teasing that others, and here the distinction between reality and invention, and perhaps we might say between fact and fiction, become blurred. Davis herself addresses some of the difficulties of definition in interview with *The Paris Review*:

> Back in the early eighties, I realized that you could write a story that was really just a narration of something that had happened to you, and change it slightly, without having really to fictionalize it. In a way, that's found material. I think it's hard to draw the line and say that something isn't found material. Because if a friend of mine tells me a story or a dream, I guess that's found material. If I get an e-mail that lends itself to a good story, that's found material. But then if I notice the cornmeal making little condensations, is that found material? It's my own, I'm not using text, but I am using a situation that exists. I'm not making it up. I find what happens in reality very interesting and I don't find a great need to make up things, but I do like retelling stories that are told to me. [Lydia Davis, 'Art of Fiction' Interview]

Davis loves to recycle the lived experience, then, and often talks about taking notes as she moves through her day, always alive to the possibilities of art in life. Her work often makes us wonder where life ends and art begins, and whether or not this is a distinction that can be made at all.

28

Davis and the Lived Experience: Letters of Complaint

LIFE CAN BECOME ART SO EASILY, then, and this can be seen also in some of her stories that take the form of letters. Often these begin as serious queries or complaints, but which gradually take on the patina of art. There are several of these in the collection *Can't and Won't*, for instance, including 'Letter to a Marketing Manager', about a biographical mistake in a newsletter; 'Letter to the President of the American Biographical Institute, Inc.', which is a response to a mistake in the spelling of Davis's name; and 'Letter to the Foundation', one of the longest, which is a letter to an institution that has awarded her a grant, discussing how the award has affected her life. Another excellent example of this kind of story is 'Letter To a Frozen Peas Manufacturer', quoted here in full:

Dear Frozen Peas Manufacturer,
We are writing to you because we feel that the peas illustrated on your package of frozen peas are a most unattractive color. We are referring to the 16 oz. plastic package that shows three or four pods, one of them split open, with peas rolling out near them. The peas are a dull yellow green, more the color of pea soup than fresh peas and nothing like the actual color of your peas, which are a nice bright dark green. The depicted peas are, moreover, about three times the size of the actual peas inside the package, which, together with their dull color, makes them even less appealing – they appear to be past their maturity and mealy in texture. Additionally, the color of your illustrated peas contrasts poorly with the color of the lettering and other decoration on your package, which is an almost harsh neon green. We have compared your depiction of peas to that of other frozen peas packages and yours is by far the least appealing. Most food manufacturers depict food on their packaging that is more attractive than the food inside and therefore deceptive. You are doing the opposite: you are falsely representing your peas as less attractive than they actually are. We enjoy your peas and do not want your business to suffer. Please reconsider your art.

Yours sincerely [*Can't and Won't*, 32]

Davis has explained in many interviews that this began as a genuine letter to a frozen peas company querying what she deems their aesthetically inadequate packaging. We feel that it is written by someone with a genuine love for a particular brand of peas, and a desire to see the product thrive. The impulse that informs the need to write such a letter is what distinguishes it from most letters. Most letters of this kind are born out of anger at having been deceived by misleading packaging into thinking the product is better than it actually is: product packaging more readily overstates than understates. There is humour in this inversion, of course, but it also raises a serious moral question. The narrator considers the marketing of peas 'art', so does that mean that companies who produce packaging that successfully manages to *overstate* the quality of their peas have done well? If this company is being chastised for doing poorly, doesn't it follow the others should be praised for managing to deceive people effectively? Davis's work thrives on such contradictions, and of course on the appealing, humorous eccentricity of characters who go to the trouble of writing such letters in the first place!

29

Recycled Experience: Lydia Davis's Dreams

Davis's collection, *Can't and Won't*, also contains a number of stories labelled 'dream' pieces. She tells us in the acknowledgements that these 'were composed from actual night dreams and dreamlike waking experiences of my own [and] of family and friends' [*Can't and Won't*, 289], and goes on to thank specific people as sources for specific dream stories. While it is appropriate that she should acknowledge her sources when they originate with other people, it is less obvious why Davis bothers to tell us in the case of her own dreams. Given the occasionally surreal nature of her stories generally, it would be hard to distinguish them from her dreams had she chosen to keep it to herself. Calling something a dream is a risky business for storytellers because it has the potential to discourage readers – other people's dreams are notoriously unappealing after all! As one reviewer quipped, 'Turns out,

Lydia Davis's dreams are just as boring as your roommate's,[22] and one can't help but wonder why Davis left herself open to such comments. But the compulsion to draw attention to their origin is interesting, particularly seeing as she takes the trouble to make the further distinction between conventional 'night' dreams, and 'dreamlike waking experiences'. While I'm not entirely sure what the latter are (I don't recall ever having such experiences myself), it has the effect of complicating rather than clarifying the difference between dream and reality. This may well be her intention, perhaps seeking to hint at how one may seep in to the other, which is of course the case, particularly for fiction writers who frequently work at the borders of reality and unreality, and for whom the unconscious often plays a significant role. One piece in which dream, reality, and fiction appear to intersect is, 'Two Characters in a Paragraph', quoted here in full:

> The story is only two paragraphs long. I'm working on the end of the second paragraph, which is the end of the story. I'm intent on this work, and my back is turned. And while I am working on the end, look what they're up to in the beginning! And they're not very far away! He seems to have drifted from where I put him and is hovering over her, only one paragraph away (in the first paragraph). True, it is a dense paragraph, and they're in the middle of it, and it's dark in there. I knew they were both in there, but when I left it and turned to the second paragraph, there wasn't anything going on between them. Now look …
> [*Can't and Won't*, 217]

This is one of Davis's own dreams, and it is interesting that it should address a loss of control over characters in a story she is writing. We have seen how a desire for control and certainty inform many of her characters' lives, and this seems to extend to their creator and her unconscious! The characters take on a life of their own here, which in a sense is the case with all characters as soon as they enter a reader's mind; certainly authors cannot control how they will signify to potential readers. So perhaps this story expresses her unease about her writing's potential reception, the idea that she cannot ultimately control how her characters will be perceived and understood? Having said this, the narrator does seem quite sanguine about her characters' transgression, and the tone is very playful. This is particularly evident in the ending where readers are forced to speculate about the exact nature of the characters' behaviour, and are left comically frustrated by the invitation to 'look' at what they cannot see.

30

Lydia Davis and Zen: 'New Year's Resolution'

LYDIA DAVIS HAS AN INTEREST IN Zen Buddhism, and some of her stories clearly explore the concept of Zen, and perhaps even exhibit a Zen philosophy themselves. One story addressing Zen directly is 'New Year's Resolution', from *Samuel Johnson is Indignant*. Here the narrator tells us that she asked a friend, Bob, about his New Year's resolution, and he answered with a fairly standard response: 'to drink less, to lose weight'. In reply she tells him, 'I have been studying Zen philosophy again', and hence *her* New Year's resolution is, 'to learn to see myself as nothing'. [*Collected Stories*, 354] To see oneself as 'nothing' is the ambition of the Zen student, of course, who needs to find ways of circumventing or negating the ego in order to attain a sense of unity with the universe, and thereby achieve enlightenment. But immediately the narrator begins to worry that stating this intention to Bob might be a little 'competitive', seeing that his resolution was so mundane by comparison. Competitiveness suggests ego-related ambition, at odds with the aim of Zen, and this would be to undermine her resolution. Then she begins to worry about her upbringing and her history of having been encouraged to have an ego in the first place. She has been brought up to see herself as 'something', so how will it ever be possible to overcome this? How can she ever see 'something' as 'nothing'? She tells us that, 'You spend the first half of your life learning that you are something after all, now you have to spend the second half learning to see yourself as nothing'. [355] The problem has another dimension too. As soon as you accept the Zen ambition of ego-negation, seeing yourself as nothing becomes a positive ambition; it becomes, in a manner of speaking, *something*. She demonstrates that contradiction in a lovely comic line: 'You have been a negative nothing, now you want to be a positive nothing.' Confused by this apparent opposition, she qualifies her Zen aspirations in the final line of the story, with another humorous comment: 'Maybe for now I should just try, each day, to be a little less than I usually am'. [355] There is more than one way to view this. It could be seen as failure – an admission that ego-negation is beyond the narrator; it could even be viewed as satirical, sending-up the absurdity of the aspiration, and the philosophy of Zen itself. But, given the paradoxical nature of Zen, it could also be associated with success. In a manner of speaking, by identifying her inadequacies the narrator is one step closer to ego-negation; and by identifying the paradoxical implications of the ambition, she is now more likely to achieve it. This is the case because Zen is at odds with conventional reason and logic, for exactly the reasons Davis identifies in the story. A student of Zen can only hope to achieve ego-negation once they have identified and accepted the paradox at the heart of the endeavour. Zen teachers very often use humour to help students free themselves from the constraints of rational thinking, and there is a sense in which that happens here. The apparent logical impasse that Davis identifies must be embraced and transcended, and one way of doing that is by laughing at it. In other words, humour has the potential to deconstruct the logic that supports those contradictions that inhibit the narrator's need to collapse the ego.

According to the Zen scholar, Conrad Hyers, humour often features in Zen teaching 'as a technique for reversing and collapsing categories [and] embracing opposites', even becoming 'an expression of enlightenment, liberation, and inner harmony.'[23] It is clear that Davis's story also brings together two opposing philosophical positions: Western rationalism, on the one hand, and Zen on the other. The effect, as so often in Zen humour according to Myers, is to 'point up the absurdity in trying to grasp after and cling to reality by means of this or that philosophical position'. [271] Very often Davis's writing, and her humour, can be seen to be in the spirit of Zen for exactly this reason. It interrogates the mechanisms that we use to understand the world – like narrative, language, logic, and reason – in order to expose their limitations.

31

Lydia Davis and Zen: 'The Cows'

ANOTHER PIECE WITH A ZEN DIMENSION is her long short story, 'The Cows', which appears in the collection *Can't and Won't*, but which was also published separately in 2011 by Sarabande Books. This is based on Davis's observations of her neighbour's cows grazing in a nearby field, and she has her narrator detail the movements of these animals over the course of time. The narrator depicts their behaviour meticulously, using deadpan prose that focuses exclusively on the animals.

> She moos toward the wooded hills behind her, and the sound comes back. She moos in a high falsetto before the note descends abruptly, or she moos in a falsetto that does not descend. It is a very small sound to come from such a large, dark animal. [*Can't and Won't*, 124]

The narrator relates their uncomplicated, inscrutable, utterly unself-conscious behaviour in a way that is weirdly captivating, despite the apparent mundanity of the subject. As described here, the cows appear completely at one with their existence. The simplicity and matter-of-factness of the prose mirrors the simplicity of their life and actions, and often the narrator almost seems at one with her subject – the distance between narrator and beasts appears to collapse, and we can imagine her achieving a Zen-like emptying of the self as she observes and narrates. Of course this is an illusion, as Davis herself points out in interview. While she admits to envying their empty minds, there is no way the experience facilitates enlightenment for her: 'I appear to be standing still, just observing them, but since it is written over a certain time, I am only standing still for a moment to observe them, so I haven't yet achieved what they have achieved.'[24] This is another text which explores Davis's interest in the egoless experience, then, in this case through an observation of the natural world. Humour also plays a part in this story, albeit in a less obvious way. The narrator's preoccupation with the routine behaviour of cows is potentially amusing in itself, but this is compounded by our developing sense of the pointlessness of their lives, underscored by Davis via expertly timed phrasing and repetitions – notice, for instance, how her reiteration of the word 'moos' in the extract above generates a humorous tone in the narrative (this is particularly noticeable when the piece is read aloud). When the cow moos toward the hills we are told that the 'sound comes back', which accentuates our sense of the inexplicability of the cows' existence, and, given that her response is to moo again, their unquestioning acceptance of it, and willingness to continue with life despite it; they are content, in other words, and the narrator's own appreciation of that contentment is implied by her patient willingness to delineate their lives, and reveal what we might term, the significance of the insignificant. A Zen reading of this story would of course encourage us to learn from the cows.[25]

32

Lydia Davis and Zen: 'Collaboration with Fly' and 'Sitting with My Little Friend'

A ZEN-LIKE HUMOUR ALSO SEEMS at work in some of Davis's shortest pieces, like 'Collaboration with Fly' from the collection *Varieties of Disturbance* (2007), quoted here in full:

> I put that word on the page,
> but he added the apostrophe. [*Collected Stories*, 508]

Here the transformation of a fly into an apostrophe creates a pleasingly incongruous comic image that seems born of a desire to collapse the distinction between human and non-human. The fly changes the meaning without meaning to. By constructing the fly as an apostrophe the narrator allows it to share in the making of meaning, thereby perhaps undermining the author-ego as a source of that meaning. At the same time, Davis might also be questioning the ultimate possibility of significance: in what sense can a statement created by a 'collaboration' between human and insect have meaning at all? By comically subverting the human/insect hierarchy Davis is once more 'collapsing categories [and] embracing opposites' in a piece which de-privileges the human ego.

As seen in 'The Cows', Davis occasionally celebrates and even seems to envy the instinctiveness of animals – their lack of self-consciousness and their at-oneness with the moment. Consider also, 'Sitting with My Little Friend', again quoted in full:

> Sitting with my little friend in the sunshine on the front step:
> I am reading a book by Blanchot
> and she is licking her leg. (*Can't and Won't*, 256)

The author of the book referenced here, Maurice Blanchot (1907-2003), is a French philosopher, and there is a sense in which the speaker's highbrow pursuit is qualified by the unpretentious and instinctive behaviour of her 'Little Friend'. The latter may be a pet of some kind, but we cannot be sure: it could possibly be a child, or perhaps even a diminutive adult. Either way, the simplicity of the animal/childlike like behaviour is juxtaposed with an elevated human pursuit of meaning, and the latter is comically qualified by the former. Because 'she' is not identified, the story won't allow us to distinguish between human and animal, and hence that distinction is collapsed too.

33

The End of the Story

LYDIA DAVIS'S ONLY NOVEL SO FAR, *The End of the Story*, was published in 1995. It explores some of the themes addressed in her shorter fiction, most notably perhaps the themes of storytelling and obsession. Indeed, Davis's early piece, 'Story', almost tells the story of the novel in microcosm: as we saw earlier, in this piece a narrator obsesses over her absent lover, as is the case in another early story, 'The Letter', which also deals with similar events and states of mind. Both were clearly inspired by the same experiences that inform her novel, which Davis admits is heavily autobiographical. According to Christopher J. Knight, they refer to a period in the 1980s when Davis was working as a visiting writer at the University of California, San Diego. As well as Davis as the unnamed narrator, the novel features many of Davis's colleagues and friends, including the critic Michael Davidson, and the writer Edith Jarolim, who appear in the book as the narrator's friends

Mitchell and Ellie.[26]

The novel is about the narrator's struggle to come to terms with, and write about, the breakdown of a brief affair she had with a 22-year-old man when she was 35. She describes the meeting, breakup, and emotional fallout with forensic detail, but the story itself is mostly eclipsed by the narrator's account of the problems she has actually telling it in a way that satisfies her. In this respect the novel has been described a commentary on the process of writing a novel, rather than as a novel as such. As Hilton Als writes, 'Davis has written a brilliant essay in the form of a novel – a work that is concerned less with the story itself than with the compulsion to tell it'. [Quoted in Knight, 201] So we can see clear similarities between this and stories like, 'The Center of the Story', and 'What Was Interesting'. Davis involves us in the process of presenting her story, and the issues that her attempts to render lived experiences raise about accuracy and emotional integrity. It is a very self-conscious story in other words, one which constantly pauses to reflect on the process of telling, the possibility of truth in narrative, and the limitations of the medium in which she must work as a writer.

34

Structuring the Story of
The End of the Story

THE NOVEL BEGINS WITH WHAT THE narrator feels is the end of the story: the point when her pursuit of her old lover appears to have ended. It is a point at which she is searching for her ex-lover in an unfamiliar city, and ends up in a bookshop where a man makes her a cup of tea. Having narrated this 'ending', she goes on to narrate some of the events that have led up to it. In the 'now' of the story, the narrator is married to a man named Vincent, and she shuttles between past and present in her narration, gradually unpacking the story of meeting her lover, their brief relationship, their break up, and her infatuation. As we read the book we share in the storyteller's struggles to organise her tale effectively, and one of the first problems she has concerns structure: 'I tried chronological order and that didn't work, so I tried a random order. Then the problem was how to arrange a random order so that it made sense.'[27] The problem of having the story 'make sense' to the reader is compounded by the fact that it doesn't really make sense to her, particularly as she relies on her memory to construct it, which is of course fallible. Indeed, the narrator can't even remember when she fell in love with her young lover in the first place:

> I say at one point that I fell in love with him quite suddenly, and that it happened when we were staring at each other by candlelight. But this seems too easy, and I also can't remember just what candlelight I was talking about. There was no candlelight in the café the first evening, and there was no candlelight in my house later that night either, so evidently I don't mean I fell in love with him the first night. [45]

And while the beginning is unclear, the ending is arbitrary: she chooses to call the scene where she drinks tea in the bookshop the end, but she admits that she has imposed this on events herself, principally because she has to end it somewhere in order to give the story shape. It gives it shape for her, she tells us, because the tea-making constitutes a form of ceremony: 'the offer of a cup of tea became a ceremonial act', and she 'needed an act of ceremony in order to end the story'; in reality, however, there are ways in which 'the story went on afterward', [236] and the ending that she chooses isn't the ending at all. It stresses how reconstructing events into a coherent narrative is an artificial act involving selections and omissions which invariably distort the truth.

35

The End of the Story and the Impossibility of Truth

EVEN THOUGH SHE STRIVES TO BE truthful, she finds that she is forced to manipulate events and change them in various ways:

> I see that I am shifting the truth around a little, at certain points accidentally, but at others deliberately. I am rearranging what actually happened so that it is not only less confusing and more believable, but also more acceptable or palatable. [108]

It seems odd that one should have to rearrange the truth in order to make it more believable, but this is a phenomenon that most people who have ever tried to tell a complex story will be familiar with. When reality is recontextualised in narrative elements are lost and emphases shift, and the narrator must try and compensate for this; she must also give salience and clarity to what she feels are the important events – in other words she needs to focus on what she feels is the story, and leave everything else out. But where does the story end and the rest of reality begin? When do her experiences stop being part of her story, and become superfluous? As she says at one stage, another, completely different story could be created from the material that she has omitted: 'everything surrounding the story, everything I am leaving out of it, would make another story, or even several others, quite different in character from this one'. [63] And of course, anyone who knows a little about Lydia Davis's life at the time when this story was taking place will know that there are crucial aspects of her life that are indeed completely omitted. For instance, she presents herself as a single woman despite the fact that she had two children in her life at periods covered in the story. This does not make the story a lie, just reinforces the point that it is not, and can never be the whole story. Most importantly, perhaps, the story is shaped by partiality, and the fact that she was immersed in, and emotionally engaged with the events that she is trying to reconstruct for us. This inevitably influences how they are told; indeed she tells us at one point that she doesn't really know who her lover was, 'I don't really know what sort of person he was […] because I never saw him from the outside. I only ever knew him half a day before I was too close to see him from the outside'. [176] The proximity of her subject, and the intimacy of their relationship makes an objective assessment impossible because the narrator's emotional engagement will always influence the description:

If I am angry, he will seem shallow, cruel, and conceited; and if I am soft and tender, he will seem faithful, honest, and sensitive. The centre is missing, the original is gone. [176]

She cannot render the original partly because all that she can present are her responses to the original, and these are constantly in flux, dependent on her own moods. In these circumstances it is surely impossible to talk about truth.

36

The End of the Story and the Philosophical Novel

IT CAN BE SEEN THEN THAT *The End of the Story* is a very different kind of novel. It is postmodern in its refusal to acknowledge the possibility of truth, or indeed the efficacy of realism as a means of representing the world authentically. In its self-conscious and self-reflexive way, it strives for a more authentic way of telling, one that acknowledges the limitations of narrative. As Knight suggests, it is in keeping with the sentiments expressed by several theorists about the inadequacy of conventional fiction, including Giles Gunn's observation:

> That the artist as artist is no longer centrally in touch with the most representative of seminal experience of our time and that this experience is no longer necessarily susceptible to being rendered in more traditional fictive forms. In fact, there seems to be at work in literary culture an active belief to the contrary: that the only forms capable

of fully and accurately rendering the ironic, disjunctive, self-contradictory character of contemporary experience are critical, recursive, ratiocinative, and highly self-reflexive, just because the characteristic experience of our time centres on the human mind itself as it moves in brilliant but sometimes fitful and ever more disbelieving steps toward the end of its own tether. [Quoted in Knight, 221-222]

In this respect *The End of the Story* takes its lead from early postmodernist texts such as John Barth's *Lost in the Funhouse* (1968), which, like Davis's novel, includes a narrator who constantly interrupts the narrative to reflect on the problems of telling the story. It has similarities also with the work of writers such as Philip Roth, who in books like *My Life as a Man* (1975) and *The Facts* (1989), addresses very similar problems to Davis: in the former a novelist finds that he cannot tell a 'true' story in a way that satisfies himself or his readers, whilst in the latter, a fiction writer – Roth himself – offers a 'factual' version of his life only to have that undermined by one of his own fictional characters, who steps into the book to find fault with everything he presents as 'true'. It also anticipates the self-conscious tone of books such as *Atonement* (2001) by the British author Ian McEwan, which also focuses on a writer's manipulation of facts. These texts in various ways capture the spirit of irony and self-contradiction that Gunn identifies. It is writing that, according to theorists like Patricia Waugh, constitutes 'both a response and contribution to an even more thoroughgoing sense that reality or history are provisional: no longer a world of eternal verities but a series of constructions, artifices, impermanent structures.'[28] Certainly the world that Davis's narrator sees is 'provisional' in that it's always beyond her ability to render it. The 'eternal verities' such as a belief in stable characters and unproblematic recollection of events are exposed as illusory in a novel where nothing is fully under the author's control: 'It isn't turning out the way I thought it would,' she tells us near the end of her narrative, 'I don't know how much control I ever really had over it'. [197]

While *The End of the Story* is a short novel, it is by far the longest original work that Davis has produced to date, and, as suggested, it embodies many of her preoccupations as a writer, and the issues explored throughout her shorter works. To some degree the novel hasn't received the attention it deserves, having been eclipsed by the success of her *Collected Stories*, and her profile as a short story writer. However, it is a highly accomplished book which interrogates its themes with characteristic scrupulosity and wit.

37

Conclusion

IT WAS SUGGESTED EARLIER DAVIS HAS been perceived by many as a writer's writer, and it can be seen how such themes as the possibility of truth in writing are of interest to authors. She explores such concerns with intelligence, and the insight of an obsessive practitioner. Despite the fact that she was a little known author until comparatively recently, her impact on fellow writers has been immense. Writing in 2010, for instance, Emily Stokes says the following:

> Today, Davis occupies a very particular place in American letters, being both one of the most respected writers in America and, until recently, when her collected stories were published in a pleasing tangerine-coloured hardback, relatively unknown. Lorin Stein has compared her to the Velvet Underground, saying that, although their first LP sold only a few thousand copies, everybody who bought one went out and started a band; Davis has similarly

influenced a generation of writers including Jonathan Franzen, David Foster Wallace, and Dave Eggers, who wrote that Davis 'blows the roof off of so many of our assumptions about what constitutes short fiction'. Rick Moody has described her as 'the best prose stylist in America'.[29]

Since winning the International Booker Prize in 2013 her profile is much higher, of course, and her influence continues to spread. This may be particularly the case among exponents of the short form, as her career parallels the rise in popularity of so-called micro or flash fiction. While very short fiction has existed for as long as storytelling itself, recent years have witnessed an increase in the production of miniature narrative forms, with their popularity linked to, among other things, the emergence of the internet and small screen consumption. It is easy to see Davis as a pioneer in this sense, particularly given the enthusiasm she has for miniature narrative, and her tireless willingness to explore its possibilities. While her stories are varied, often resembling anecdotes, fables, jokes, parables, prose poems, and everything in between, many are impossible to easily categorise, and can only be assessed on their own terms. In this respect she is as an important innovator, and Craig Morgan Teicher's often quoted assessment doesn't feel like an exaggeration: 'Lydia Davis is the master of a literary form largely of her own invention.'[30] It demands a certain amount of bravery and conviction to invent a form, and to follow one's instincts as a writer for the duration of one's career. As suggested at the outset of this book, something she admires about the Norwegian Dag Solstad is his determination to 'do what [he] wants' as a writer, and Davis is driven by similar convictions and bravery. But form is nothing without content, and it is Davis's ability to shed fresh light on the human experience that makes her an important writer. The English novelist Ali Smith addresses this aspect of her achievement in her discussion of Davis as her own personal hero: 'It's all about how you read and about the reflorescence of what and how things mean with Davis.'[31] As we have seen, Davis's perception of the world is one that forces us to rethink our assumptions: whether this is our assumptions about animals, autobiography, cows, identity, language, obsession, originality, reading stories, writing stories, translating stories, or Zen. Davis has her narrators explore these themes in ways that question what we thought we knew about them. While the result of that questioning might often be postmodern uncertainty, the act of interrogation involves a creative 'reflorescence' that encourages new ways of thinking, and potential new meanings to blossom.

38

Selected Bibliography

Books by Lydia Davis

The Thirteenth Woman and Other Stories, New York: Living Hand, 1976

Sketches for a Life of Wassilly, Station Hill Press, 1981.

Story and Other Stories, Great Barrington, MA: The Figures, 1985

Break It Down, New York: Knopf, 1986

The End of the Story, New York: Farrar, Straus & Giroux, 1995

Almost No Memory, New York: Farrar, Straus & Giroux, 1997

Samuel Johnson Is Indignant, New York: McSweeney's, 2001

Varieties of Disturbance, New York: Farrar, Straus & Giroux, May 2007

Proust, Blanchot, and a Woman in Red,
   Center for Writers and Translators, *2007*
The Collected Stories of Lydia Davis, New York:
   Farrar, Straus & Giroux, 2009
The Cows, Sarabande Books, 2011
Can't and Won't: Stories, New York:
   Farrar, Straus and Giroux, 2014

Selected Translations by Lydia Davis

Jean Chesneaux, Françoise Le Barbier,
   Marie-Claire Bergère, *China from the 1911
   Revolution to Liberation*. Translators Paul Auster
   and Lydia Davis. Hassocks: Harvester Press, 1977

Georges Simenon, *African Trio*, Translators Paul Auster,
   Lydia Davis. Stuart Gilbert. London:
   Hamish Hamilton, 1979

Maurice Blanchot, P. Adams Sitney, ed.
   The Gaze of Orpheus and Other Literary Essays.
   Translator Lydia Davis. Station Hill Press, 1981

Françoise Giroud, *Marie Curie: A Life*.
   Translator Lydia Davis. Holmes & Meier, 1986

Michel Leiris, *Scratches*, Translator Lydia Davis.
   Baltimore and London: Johns Hopkins University
   Press, 1991

Jean Pierre Jouve, *Vagadu*. Translator Lydia Davis.
   Evanston: Marlboro/Northwestern University Press, 1997

Marcel Proust, *Swann's Way*. Translator Lydia Davis. London: Allen Lane, 2002

Gustave Flaubert, *Madame Bovary*. Translator Lydia Davis. New York: Viking, Penguin, 2010

Secondary Sources:
Selected Criticism and Critical Interviews

Andrea Aguilar and Johanne Fronth-Nygren, 'Interview With Lydia Davis', Art of Fiction No. 227, *Paris Review*, Issue 212, Spring 2015, https://www.theparisreview.org/interviews/6366/lydia-davis-art-of-fiction-no-227-lydia-davis

Karen Alexander, 'Breaking it Down: Analysis in the Stories of Lydia Davis', in Ellen Burton Harrington (ed.) *Scribbling Women & The Short Story Form: Approaches by American & British Women Writers*, New York, Frankfurt: Lang, 2008, 165-77

Josh Cohen, 'Reflexive Incomprehension: on Lydia Davis', *Textual Practice*, 24, 3, 501-16

Jonathan Evans, *The Many Voices of Lydia Davis: Translation, Rewriting, Intertextuality*, Edinburgh: Edinburgh University Press, 2016

Nettie Farris, '"I Try to Figure It Out"; "Maybe the Answer Is What Will Occur to Me Later, When I Look Back": Reconciliation and Ceremonial Closure in the Fiction of Lydia Davis', *Journal of Kentucky Studies*, 30, 2013, 122-128

Ane Farsethas, 'Lydia Davis at the End of the World: On Learning Norwegian and Writing the Beauty of the Dying World', *The Literary Hub*, 9 April 2015, http://lithub.com/lydia-davis-at-the-end-of-the-world/

Christopher J. Knight, 'Lydia Davis's Own Philosophical Investigation: *The End of the Story*', *Journal of Narrative Theory*, 38, 2, Summer 2008, 198-228

Larry McCaffery, 'Deliberately, Terribly Neutral: An Interview with Lydia Davis', in Larry McCaffery (ed.), *Some Other Frequency: Interviews with Innovative American Authors*, Philadelphia: University of Pennsylvania Press, 1996, 59-79

Marjorie Perloff, 'Fiction as Language Game: The Hermeneutic Parables of Lydia Davis and Maxine Chernoff', in Ellen G. Friedman and Miriam Fuchs (eds.), *Breaking the Sequence: Women's Experimental Fiction*, Princeton: Princeton University Press, 1989, 199-214

David Winters, 'Like Sugar Dissolving: *On The End of the Story* by Lydia Davis', *The Quarterly Conversation*, 10 March 2014 http://quarterlyconversation.com/likesugar-dissolving on-the-end-of-the-story-by-lydia-davis

Melora Wolff, 'Eye of the Storm', *Salmagundi*, Fall 2011/Winter 2012, 158-215

Endnotes

1 Dana Goodyear, 'Long Story Short: Lydia Davis's Radical Fiction', *The New Yorker*, 17 March 2014
http://www.newyorker.com/magazine/2014/03/17/long-story-short

2 See 'Fellows Brunch at the Kelly Writers House', interview conducted 25 April 2017. This is one of many recorded interviews with Davis available at the University of Pennsylvania, Center for Programs in Contemporary Writing. http://writing.upenn.edu/pennsound/x/Davis.php

3 See Jonathan Evans, *The Many Voices of Lydia Davis: Translation, Rewriting, Intertextuality*, Edinburgh: Edinburgh University Press, 2016. All future references will be to this edition.

4 See Lydia Davis, Interview with *Believer*, 2008
www.believermag.com/issues/200801/?read=interview_davis

5 Lydia Davis, *The Collected Stories of Lydia Davis*, London: Penguin Books, 2013, 155. All future references will be to this edition.

6 Ane Farsethas, 'Lydia Davis at the End of the World: On Learning Norwegian and Writing the Beauty of the Dying World', *The Literary Hub*, 9 April 2015
http://lithub.com/lydia-davis-at-the-end-of-the-world/

7 Lydia Davis, Interview with Brendan Mathews, *Salon*, Tuesday 29 April 2014
http://www.salon.com/2014/04/28/lydia_davis_i_kind_of_like_the_fact_that_my_work_isn%E2%80%99t_for_everybody/

8 Dan Chiasson, 'New York Review: *The Collected Stories of Lydia Davis*', Huffpost, 25 May 2011 www.huffingtonpost.com/2010/04/09/new-york-review-the-colle_n_531411.html

9 Lydia Davis, Interview with *The Harlequin*, 2017 www.theharlequin.org

10 Lydia Davis, Interviewed by Andrea Aguilar and Johanne Fronth-Nygren, Art of Fiction No. 227, *Paris Review*, Issue 212, Spring 2015 https://www.theparisreview.org/interviews/6366/lydia-davis-art-of-fiction-no-227-lydia-davis

11 William Skidelsky, Lydia Davis: 'My style is a reaction to Proust's long sentences', *The Guardian*, Sunday 1 August 2010 https://www.theguardian.com/books/2010/aug/01/lydia-davis-interview-reaction-proust

12 For a discussion of the categories and terminology associated with miniature fictions see Paul McDonald, *The Enigmas of Containment: The History and Poetics of Flash Fiction*, Greenwich Exchange Publishing, 2018

13 Lydia Davis, 'Form as a Response to Doubt', in Robert Cohen and Jay Parini (eds.), *The Writer's Reader*, London: Bloomsbury, 2017, 323, 323-325

14 Melora Wolff, 'Eye of the Storm', *Salmagundi*, Fall 2011/Winter 2012, 158-215, 160

15 Lydia Davis, *Can't and Won't*, London: Hamish Hamilton, 2014, 112. All future references will be made to this edition.

16 Anonymous, Review of *Almost no Memory*, *Publisher's Weekly*, 6 February 1997 www.publishersweekly.com/978-0-374-10281-4

17 David Foster Wallace, 'Laughing with Kafka', *Harper's Magazine*, July 1998, 26, 23-27 https://harpers.org/wp-content/uploads/HarpersMagazine-1998-07-0059612.pdf

18 Nathan Ihara, 'Lydia Davis's Short, Weird Fiction', *L.A. Weekly*, 30 May 2007 http://www.laweekly.com/arts/lydia-davis-short-weird-fiction-2149068

19 Siddhartha Deb, 'Just So Stories', *The New York Times*, 27 May 2007 www.nytimes.com/2007/05/27/books/review/Deb-t.html

20 Paul Auster, *Collected Prose*, London: Faber and Faber, 2003, 243-265

21 Mary Stewart Atwell and Alison Espach, 'Little Plots of Real Life: A Conversation with Lydia Davis', *Fiction Writers Review*, 24 May 2009 http://fictionwritersreview.com/interview/little-plots-of-real-life-a-conversation-with-lydia-davis-interview/

22 Chloe Schama, 'Lydia Davis Is the Perfect Writer for the Twitter Era', *New Republic*, 7 April 2014
https://www.newrepublic.com/article/117286/lydia-davis-cant-and-wont-review

23 Conrad Hyers, 'Humour and Zen: Comic Midwifery', *Philosophy East and West*, Volume 39, no. 3, July 1989, 267-277, 270

24 Lydia Davis interviewed by Christian Lund, August 2014 at the Louisiana Museum, Denmark
https://vimeo.com/107689734

25 A worthwhile reading of this story is offered by Hollis Camps, 'Human Perspective in Lydia Davis's "The Cows"', *Modern American Authors*, University of Virginia, Spring 2014
http://www.ericrettberg.com/modernamericanauthors/?p=782

26 Christopher J. Knight, 'Lydia Davis's Own Philosophical Investigation: *The End of the Story*', *Journal of Narrative Theory*, 38, 2, Summer 2008, 198-228, 200

27 Lydia Davis, *The End of the Story*, London: Penguin Books, 2015, 52. All subsequent references will be to this edition.

28 Patricia Waugh, *Metafiction: The Theory and Practice of Self-Conscious Fiction*, Routledge, 1984, 7

29 Emily Stokes, 'Lunch with the FT: Lydia Davis', *Financial Times*, 7 August 2010
https://www.ft.com/content/5c1059dc-a0ea-11df-badd-00144feabdc0

30 Craig Morgan Teicher, *The Cleveland Plain Dealer*, 12 October 2009
http://www.cleveland.com/books/index.ssf/2009/10/lydia_davis_defies_the_labels.html

31 Ali Smith, 'My hero: Lydia Davis', *The Guardian*, 24 May 2013
https://www.theguardian.com/books/2013/may/24/my-hero-lydia-davis-smith